BORIS YELTSIN

THE CHELSEA HOUSE LIBRARY OF BIOGRAPHY

BORIS YELTSIN

KATE SCHECTER

Chelsea House Publishers

New York • Philadelphia

CHELSEA HOUSE PUBLISHERS

Editorial Director Richard Rennert
Executive Managing Editor Karyn Gullen Browne
Executive Editor Sean Dolan
Copy Chief Robin James
Picture Editor Adrian G. Allen
Art Director Robert Mitchell
Manufacturing Director Gerald Levine
Systems Manager Lindsey Ottman
Production Coordinator Marie Claire Cebrián-Ume

The Chelsea House Library of Biography
Senior Editor Kathy Kuhtz

Staff for **BORIS YELTSIN**
Copy Editor Laura Petermann
Editorial Assistant Mary B. Sisson
Picture Researcher Pat Burns
Designer Basia Niemczyc
Cover Illustration Daniel O'Leary

Copyright © 1994 by Chelsea House Publishers, a division of Main Line Book Co. All rights reserved. Printed and Bound in Mexico

First Printing

1 3 5 7 9 8 6 4 2

Library of Congress Cataloging-in-Publication Data

Schecter, Kate Sara.
Boris Yeltsin/Kate Sara Schecter.
p. cm.—(Chelsea House library of biography)
Includes bibliographical references and index.
Summary: Traces the life of the Russian leader from his impoverished childhood through his political career to his role in the 1991 coup and the beginning of his presidency.
ISBN 0-7910-1749-4
    0-7910-1795-8 (pbk.)
1. Yeltsin, Boris Nikolayevich, 1931– —Juvenile literature. 2. Presidents—Russian (Federation)—Biography—Juvenile literature. [1. Yeltsin, Boris Nikolayevich, 1931–. 2. Presidents—Russia (Federation)] I. Title. II. Series.
DK290.3.Y45S34 1993   92-37474
947.085'4'092—dc20   CIP
[B]   AC

Contents

Learning from Biographies—*Vito Perrone*   7

1   Three Days That Shook the World   11

2   Fighting the Odds   27

3   The Young Rebel   37

4   A Member of the Party   49

5   The Rivals: Gorbachev and Yeltsin   61

6   The Yeltsin Affair   73

7   From Communist to Democrat   85

8   The Collapse of an Empire and the Birth of a Nation   97

Further Reading   107

Chronology   108

Index   110

THE CHELSEA HOUSE LIBRARY OF BIOGRAPHY

Barbara Bush

John C. Calhoun

Clarence Darrow

Charles Darwin

Anne Frank

William Lloyd Garrison

Martha Graham

J. Edgar Hoover

Saddam Hussein

Jesse James

Rose Kennedy

Jack London

Horace Mann

Muhammad

Edward R. Murrow

William Penn

Edgar Allan Poe

Norman Schwarzkopf

Joseph Smith

Sam Walton

Frank Lloyd Wright

Boris Yeltsin

Brigham Young

Other titles in the series are forthcoming.

Introduction

Learning from Biographies

Vito Perrone

The oldest narratives that exist are biographical. Much of what we know, for example, about the Pharaohs of ancient Egypt, the builders of Babylon, the philosophers of Greece, the rulers of Rome, the many biblical and religious leaders who provide the base for contemporary spiritual beliefs, has come to us through biographies—the stories of their lives. Although an oral tradition was long the mainstay of historically important biographical accounts, the oral stories making up this tradition became by the 1st century A.D. central elements of a growing written literature.

In the 1st century A.D., biography assumed a more formal quality through the work of such writers as Plutarch, who left us more than 500 biographies of political and intellectual leaders of Rome and Greece. This tradition of focusing on great personages lasted well into the 20th century and is seen as an important means of understanding the history of various times and places. We learn much, for example, from Plutarch's writing about the collapse of the Greek city-states and about the struggles in Rome over the justice and the constitutionality of a world empire. We also gain considerable understanding of the definitions of morality and civic virtue and how various common men and women lived out their daily existence.

Not surprisingly, the earliest American writing, beginning in the 17th century, was heavily biographical. Those Europeans who came to America were dedicated to recording their experience, especially the struggles they faced in building what they determined to be a new culture. John Norton's *Life and Death of John Cotton*, printed in 1630, typifies these early works. Later biographers often tackled more ambitious projects. Cotton Mather's *Magnalia Christi Americana*, published in 1702, accounted for the lives of more than 70 ministers and political leaders. In addition, a biographical literature around the theme of Indian captivity had considerable popularity. Soon after the American Revolution and the organization of the United States of America, Americans were treated to a large outpouring of biographies about such figures as Benjamin Franklin, George Washington, Thomas Jefferson, and Aaron Burr, among others. These particular works served to build a strong sense of national identity.

Among the diverse forms of historical literature, biographies have been over many centuries the most popular. And in recent years interest in biography has grown even greater, as biography has gone beyond prominent government figures, military leaders, giants of business, industry, literature, and the arts. Today we are treated increasingly to biographies of more common people who have inspired others by their particular acts of courage, by their positions on important social and political issues, or by their dedicated lives as teachers, town physicians, mothers, and fathers. Through this broader biographical literature, much of which is featured in the CHELSEA HOUSE LIBRARY OF BIOGRAPHY, our historical understandings can be enriched greatly.

What makes biography so compelling? Most important, biography is a human story. In this regard, it makes of history something personal, a narrative with which we can make an intimate connection. Biographers typically ask us as readers to accompany them on a journey through the life of another person, to see some part of the world through another's eyes. We can, as a result, come to understand what it is like to live the life of a slave, a farmer, a textile worker, an engineer, a poet, a president—in a sense, to walk in another's shoes. Such experience can be personally invaluable. We cannot ask for a better entry into historical studies.

Although our personal lives are likely not as full as those we are reading about, there will be in most biographical accounts many common experiences. As with the principal character of any biography, we are also faced with numerous decisions, large and small. In the midst of living our lives we are not usually able to comprehend easily the significance of our daily decisions or grasp easily their many possible consequences, but we can gain important insights into them by seeing the decisions made by others play themselves out. We can learn from others.

Because biography is a personal story, it is almost always full of surprises. So often, the personal lives of individuals we come across historically are out of view, their public personas masking who they are. It is through biography that we gain access to their private lives, to the acts that define who they are and what they truly care about. We see their struggles within the possibilities and limitations of life, gaining insight into their beliefs, the ways they survived hardships, what motivated them, and what discouraged them. In the process we can come to understand better our own struggles.

As you read this biography, try to place yourself within the subject's world. See the events as that person sees them. Try to understand why the individual made particular decisions and not others. Ask yourself if you would have chosen differently. What are the values or beliefs that guide the subject's actions? How are those values or beliefs similar to yours? How are they different from yours? Above all, remember: You are engaging in an important historical inquiry as you read a biography, but you are also reading a literature that raises important personal questions for you to consider.

Boris Yeltsin addresses the Russian Parliament in 1990 under a statue of Lenin. Yeltsin came to believe that the only way to save Russia and the other republics was to dismantle the Soviet Union and to create independent, democratic republics with free market economies.

1

Three Days That Shook the World

ON MONDAY, AUGUST 19TH, 1991, Boris Yeltsin, the president of Russia, dared to resist a coup d'état attempt to overthrow the President of the Union of Soviet Socialist Republics (USSR) by proclaiming his opposition to the coup leaders atop a tank. "Soldiers, officers, and generals," Yeltsin shouted, "the clouds of terror and dictatorship are gathering over the whole country. They must not be allowed to bring eternal night." He then declared the coup illegal, called for a general strike, and announced that any soldiers on Russian territory were subject to his orders because he had jurisdiction as the president of Russia. Later, Prime Minister John Major of Great Britain described Yeltsin's speech on top of the tank as a moment of "sheer raw courage."

The attempt to overthrow the central government marked the beginning of the end of the USSR, which dominated the world as the most

On August 19, 1991, in front of the Russian White House, Yeltsin speaks to the Muscovites—and to the world—from atop a tank, vowing to fight the coup plotters in their attempt to overthrow President Mikhail Gorbachev.

powerful Communist country for 74 years. At the time of the coup attempt, Boris Yeltsin served as the first freely elected president of Russia, the largest and most powerful of the 15 republics that made up the USSR. The president of the Soviet Union, Mikhail Gorbachev, had led the country since 1985.

During Gorbachev's years in power, a rivalry developed between Gorbachev and Yeltsin, and the attempted coup became the true test of which man would ultimately lead the country into the new post-Communist era. Yeltsin recognized that the USSR needed to change. The economic and political concepts behind communism had failed the country, and the Soviet people suffered under poor living conditions. Yeltsin understood the popular outrage against the government and used his political abilities to align himself with the people. Eventually, the Russian people would choose Yeltsin to guide Russia out of the Communist era. Yeltsin earned national prominence as a believer in his country's Communist ideology, but he gradually came to realize that the only way to save Russia and the other republics was to dismantle the Soviet Union and to create a group of independent, democratic, capitalist states with a free market economy.

Yeltsin's leadership in resisting the 1991 coup attempt catapulted him to world fame. His courage and heroic defiance of the conspirators, who wanted to impose a military dictatorship on the Soviet Union, are characteristics that have dominated Yeltsin's personality all his life. When it seemed that seven years of reforms and progress towards democracy might be crushed by the militant coup leaders, Yeltsin alone stood up and resisted the political takeover. Once Yeltsin took the first step, many followed to support him.

The damage done by the coup attempt was equal to that of a nuclear disaster or a gigantic earthquake—the USSR and Russia would never be the same after the shake-up. Not only did the leadership of the country change after the coup attempt, but a complete political and economic transformation followed as well.

When Gorbachev came to power in 1985, he initiated changes in Soviet society that led to a democratization and loosening up of what had been a repressive and controlling political system. One of Gorbachev's reforms included his social liberalization policy of *glasnost*, or openness, in which the Soviet people became free to engage in public debate. Although it was still illegal to criticize the KGB (the secret police), the Soviet military, or high-ranking officials, people could voice their opinions and influence public policy. Another of Gorbachev's reforms, his economic policy known as *perestroika*, or restructuring, involved a plan to revitalize the Soviet economy. In initiating these changes, Gorbachev allowed some political prisoners to be released, opened up previously taboo subjects to public debate, loosened censorship, allowed religious organizations and independent clubs to meet, and began to turn the country in a democratic direction. He also established new relationships with the West. The true test of a democracy, however, is its open and fair elections, and although Gorbachev started the process, he would never test his own popularity by running in an election. Poll results soon indicated that Yeltsin had the overwhelming support of the people. On June 12, 1991, the people of Russia elected Yeltsin president of their republic and he became the first leader of Russia to be chosen by popular vote.

Warning signs that trouble lurked in Gorbachev's government abounded before the August 19 coup attempt. Many Soviet citizens were disillusioned with Gorbachev. The early years of glasnost and perestroika had promised hope for a new, open society with freedom and a higher standard of living. Seven years later, political reforms allowed for more freedom of speech, but living conditions continued to worsen; many ethnic groups and people from the non-Russian republics persisted in their fight for independence from the central government in Moscow; and Gorbachev continued to be more involved with foreign policy than with domestic problems. As Gorbachev's power waned, his decrees and orders for reforms were often ignored, and his advisers hinted to him that someone might try to kill him or take over the Soviet government.

In fact, there had already been one failed attempt to assassinate Gorbachev in Moscow's Red Square in 1990. A disgruntled officer even wrote an article in a military newspaper about the need for a military takeover a few months before the coup plotters made their move. Repeatedly, Gorbachev's closest advisers warned him that a plot might be brewing and that he should take precautions, but he ignored their advice. Gorbachev had appointed every man in the upper echelons of the Soviet government, and he could not conceive of any one of them

The eight members of the State Committee for the State of Emergency hold a press conference on August 19, 1991. The conspirators represented the most influential branches of the Soviet government and included Prime Minister Valentin Pavlov (far right) and Vice-president Gennady Yanayev (speaking).

betraying him. The attempt to oust Gorbachev, perpetrated by a group of eight men, devastated him, and he never recovered his power or his confidence afterwards.

Yeltsin, on the other hand, had been far more suspicious of the men in power who pretended to be so loyal to Gorbachev, but who secretly planned to take over his authority. During the months leading up to the coup, Yeltsin began to develop strong ties with military commanders and officials in the KGB when he realized that these powerful forces did not wholly support Gorbachev's policies. At the time, Yeltsin did not intend to create a Russian army separate from the Soviet army (though this would eventually occur after the USSR disintegrated), but he did try to meet with army units after hearing the discontentment among the soldiers. On visits to army barracks, Yeltsin taught the officers and soldiers the basic ideas behind a democratic political system, and he tried to convince them that he had their welfare in mind.

The eight coup plotters, who called themselves the State Committee for the State of Emergency, represented the most powerful branches of the Soviet government and included Prime Minister Valentin Pavlov, Vice-President Gennady Yanayev, Minister of the Interior Boris Pugo, Chairman of the KGB Vladimir Kryuchkov, Minister Leonid Kravchenko (in charge of censorship), Minister of Defense Marshal Dmitri Yazov and his military colleague Oleg Baklanov, and Alexander Tizyukov, a representative of industrial interests.

Upon taking over the Kremlin on August 19, the coup leaders immediately ordered army troops in tanks to roll into Moscow to create a show of force. A group of tanks approached Yeltsin's office and awaited orders to attack. (Yeltsin had been at his dacha, or country house, at

Upon taking over the Kremlin on August 19, the coup leaders ordered army tanks into Moscow to create a show of force. The Soviet tanks pictured here are taking position outside the Kremlin (left) near the onion-shaped domes of the Cathedral of St. Basil the Blessed.

Arkhangelskoye on Monday morning, August 19, and had reached his Moscow office by late morning.) The troops sent to Yeltsin's office building, which is nicknamed the White House because of its white color and its important role of headquarters of the Russian government, awaited the signal to storm the building and to kill anyone who resisted them. Yeltsin later told reporters that the troops that surrounded the White House had been, "armed with very powerful weapons. . . . The ground floor and first floors of the building were to be subjected to a simultaneous hail of fire from all sides. A hail of fire directed at everything, to shoot at every living thing, doors, windows, everything." The soldiers also had orders to capture or kill Yeltsin and his associates and to clear the building of all people.

Yeltsin's earlier contact with officers and soldiers, however, paid off; he persuaded the army not to attack his office or the people resisting the coup. The army commanders' decision to disobey orders from the coup leaders and not to shoot at civilians helped to foil the plotters' plan—the coup only lasted three days.

The coup leaders' underestimation of Yeltsin's ability to create a powerful popular resistance turned out to be one of their biggest mistakes. Although the plotters had the KGB monitoring Yeltsin's every move before the coup, they chose not to arrest him. Yeltsin, who happened to be far away in the republic of Kazakhstan a few days before the coup, could not have fought back with such force if they had acted a few days earlier. Instead, by August 19th, Yeltsin had returned to his dacha near Moscow. Upon hearing of the coup, Yeltsin decided to try to get to the White House to plan a resistance movement. In Vladimir Solovyov and Elena Klepikova's book about Yeltsin, entitled *Boris Yeltsin: A Political Biography*, the authors report that as he got into his car his daughter Tanya said, "Don't worry, Dad. Now it all depends on you alone."

None of the tanks in the streets stopped Yeltsin from reaching the White House. When the tanks rolled into Moscow that morning, people came out of their homes and offices to see what was happening. Although the citizens appeared angry and surprised by what they saw, there was at first no resistance to the military. The country reacted similarly to the coup. People adopted a "wait and see" attitude before they put their lives on the line. Mass resistance remained scattered and occurred mostly in the two major cities of Moscow and Leningrad. Initially, Yeltsin was the sole resistor of the coup.

Yeltsin's brave and decisive actions were exactly the opposite of those displayed by the plotters. Instead of hiding in the White House and asking his colleagues for advice, Yeltsin decided to take a stand and to chance losing his life. One British reporter wrote of the valiant moment on the tank, "Yeltsin's defiance proved, if proof was needed, that he was a man who was prepared to risk his life for his beliefs. The image he had helped to create of himself, as a hero standing firm against impossible odds, was finally revealed to be more than what the Russians call *vrayno* (bragging)."

It is ironic that 74 years earlier the Bolshevik Revolution, led by Vladimir Ilich Lenin, started in a similar fashion, with Lenin standing on the barricades inciting the Russian people to fight for change and to overthrow the old order. Now Yeltsin called for an end to the years of Communist rule that the Bolsheviks had instituted. Yeltsin became the instigator of a new revolution, calling for democracy and an end to the power of the Soviet regime. The Bolshevik system of socialism that started in 1917 was coming to an end, and Yeltsin was the only leader brave enough to stand on the ramparts and proclaim his willingness to march forward, whatever the obstacles.

However, it was not only Yeltsin's bravery that helped turn the course of events. His skill as a politician helped him draw worldwide support and trick and confuse the coup leaders. Soon after the coup became known to other world leaders, especially those from western democracies, they telephoned Yeltsin at his office to voice their support for him and his struggle. When President George Bush of the United States called, Yeltsin told Bush he could not talk for long because tanks were rolling toward the Russian White House. Yeltsin's description of the seriousness of the situation created a sense of urgency and fear abroad. All eyes were on the coup leaders and the Russian army to see if they would go against international support of prodemocracy forces. Yeltsin and his associates spent most of the three days of the coup attempt on the telephone with reporters and world leaders trying to get information and relay it to other people within the Soviet Union and to the rest of the world. Later, two Russian reporters, describing the activity in the White House during the coup attempt, said, "Phones defeated tanks; words prevailed over bullets."

Yeltsin used his cunning to trick the coup leaders with false information. On the second day of the coup, he added to the disarray and indecision of the conspirators by leaking reports—made up for the sole purpose of creating confusion among the coup leaders—from the White House that some of the coup participants had given up the coup attempt and were resigning from their political positions. Yeltsin's plan worked, and later analyses of the coup revealed that the group members started out indecisive and wavering, and then rapidly fell apart when they thought the group was disintegrating. On the third day of the coup, Yeltsin convinced Kryuchkov, the chairman of the KGB, through these false reports to leave the Kremlin to travel to the Crimea to see Gorbachev. While Kryuchkov was on his way, Yeltsin arranged for his arrest. Yeltsin outwitted the eight conspirators, and in the process added to his own self-confidence and growing popularity.

Many observers believe that the coup failed because the plotters wavered in their intentions from the beginning of

Vladimir Ilich Lenin, leader of the Bolsheviks, addresses the men of Russia in a public square in Moscow. In 1917, Lenin implored the Russians to fight for change and to overthrow the exploitative government; on November 7, 1917, the Bolsheviks seized power and the Socialist Soviet government was born.

their ill-fated plan. Gennady Yanayev, the vice-president of the Soviet Union and one of the coup leaders, said at a news conference on the first day of the takeover that Gorbachev did not feel well enough to lead the country anymore. "Let me say that Mikhail Gorbachev is now on vacation: he's undergoing treatment in the south of our country. He is tired after these many years, and he will need some time to get better, and it is our hope . . . that Mikhail Gorbachev, as soon as he feels better, will resume his office again." According to Valentin Stepankov, Russia's prosecutor general who was responsible for the investigation of the coup attempt, the leaders of the coup told Kremlin doctors to draw up a medical report that would assure everyone that Gorbachev could not perform his duties—Gorbachev really was in the Crimea on vacation when the conspirators tried to depose him. In addition, Yanayev, at the news conference, had failed to add that the plotters had put Gorbachev under house arrest when they took over the Kremlin and ordered the tanks to enter Moscow.

The USSR was not a democracy like that of the United States, in which a presidential election is held every four years. Instead, every time the Soviet leadership changed, a power struggle ensued. After each shift of leadership, the new successor would make a statement in which he in effect explained that the former leader could not head the country anymore because he had taken ill. Joseph Stalin started this practice when he systematically killed off his rivals in the 1930s and 1940s, in what are now known as Stalin's purges. After an execution, an official statement would explain that the well-known dignitary had been too ill to continue working and had voluntarily retired. Everyone knew that whenever a victim of Stalin's was said to have "retired," he or she would never be seen or heard from again. Later, after Stalin's death, other Soviet leaders used the same lie to usurp power.

THREE DAYS THAT SHOOK THE WORLD

This time the old falsehood clearly bore no resemblance to the truth, and no one believed Yanayev's statement. Even Yanayev himself seemed doubtful of its validity after he announced it. Although the plotters tried to take over the Kremlin and oust Gorbachev, they did not have the confidence to proclaim a change in power and to begin a new path of governance. The coup plotters acted as a group, and they did not have an obvious leader. Besides having difficulty with making decisions about how to conduct the coup, the plotters had not even laid plans for what they would accomplish if their overthrow was a success. The group's lack of leadership, along with their inability to take a course of action and to decisively assume control over the government, cost them their positions in the Kremlin. In addition, the news conferences, and later the resistance to the coup, were all filmed live on television. The world watched as the plotters floundered in their attempts to decide how to present their case. The coup, however, did not fail only because of the conspirators' indecisiveness—Yeltsin had rallied the masses to resist them.

During the 1991 coup attempt, a woman (in foreground) climbs a tank while other demonstrators form a human chain to stop a tank column from advancing on Moscow's Gorky Street.

On August 22, Yeltsin flashes the victory sign to tens of thousands of Russians at a rally marking the end of the coup attempt. The coup conspirators unintentionally helped Yeltsin and his followers launch into a new post-Communist era.

It was as much their indecisiveness as their inability to recognize the vast changes that had taken place in communications technology that contributed to the downfall of the eight men who plotted the coup. Yeltsin used the media to fight against a return to the old order. He had traveled to the United States in 1989 and had seen how much more technologically advanced than the USSR the West had become. Unlike many of the former Communist leaders who resisted change, Yeltsin used the media to his advantage. Although the coup leaders tried to control the state-run television industry, reports of Moscow civilians setting up barricades against the approaching tanks, and interviews with people out on the streets ready to resist in any way possible, slipped onto the evening news during the coup attempt. The plotters thought they could just announce the takeover of the government and decree what could be shown on television, but in fact they had little control over the nation's broadcast and television systems, and news of the resistance quickly leaked out along with official proclamations by the coup leaders. For three days the Soviet people watched conflicting reports about the coup and about who was in control of the country. An information revolution had occurred long before the coup attempt, but the coup leaders remained blind to this and other changes in the country.

During the coup attempt, Yeltsin appeared on television and implored the "soldiers and officers of Russia" to "not let yourselves be turned into blind weapons to defend privileges. In this difficult hour, distinguish real truth from lies. Do not dishonor Russia by shedding the blood of your own people. The days of plotters are numbered. Law and constitutional order will be victorious. Russia will be free." Yeltsin exuded confidence that the will of the people would prevail.

By the third day of the coup, the plan to take over the Kremlin had unraveled. The plotters were arrested while trying to leave Moscow. Yeltsin sent two of his supporters to bring Gorbachev and his family back to Moscow, and many of the leaders of the other republics (who were silent during the coup) rushed to condemn the attempted overthrow and to join sides with Yeltsin.

Three young men killed in conflicts with the army in Moscow and the suicide of Boris Pugo (he shot his wife, who later died, before killing himself when he realized the coup had failed) were the human casualties of the coup. However, bloodshed remained relatively low considering the potentially explosive nature of the situation. During the tense hours of August 19–20, many of the soldiers who drove the tanks expressed their reluctance to point guns at their own people. Hundreds of muscovites showed their resistance by sticking flowers in gun barrels and bringing food to the soldiers, who had to sit in their tanks for three consecutive days.

Gorbachev returned to Moscow, badly shaken after the coup attempt. His reputation as leader of the Soviet Union had been severely undermined. Gorbachev had appointed the men involved in the coup to their posts and he had trusted them. Now his judgment was put into question. After the coup attempt, Gorbachev admitted that his efforts to maintain the old system alongside the new freedoms he had initiated could not work. As one critic of the Soviet system phrased it earlier, communism and democracy are like "fried snowballs"—they are incompatible.

The failed coup sped up the process of democratization that had begun months earlier. Instead of stopping the creation of a freer, more open society, the coup plotters inadvertently helped Yeltsin and the supporters of demsocracy to bring about a new post-Communist era. People toppled statues of Bolshevik leaders, such as Lenin, and the crumbling Soviet government soon collapsed completely. The Communist party, the only political party allowed to exist under communism, became illegal, and with its demise the centralizing force that held the Soviet Union together also broke down. By the end of 1991, the Soviet Union no longer existed. Gorbachev resigned in

Angry Muscovites topple a statue of Feliks Dzerzhinski, founder of the KGB security police, outside the KGB's headquarters on August 23. After the attempted coup, the Soviet government soon disintegrated completely.

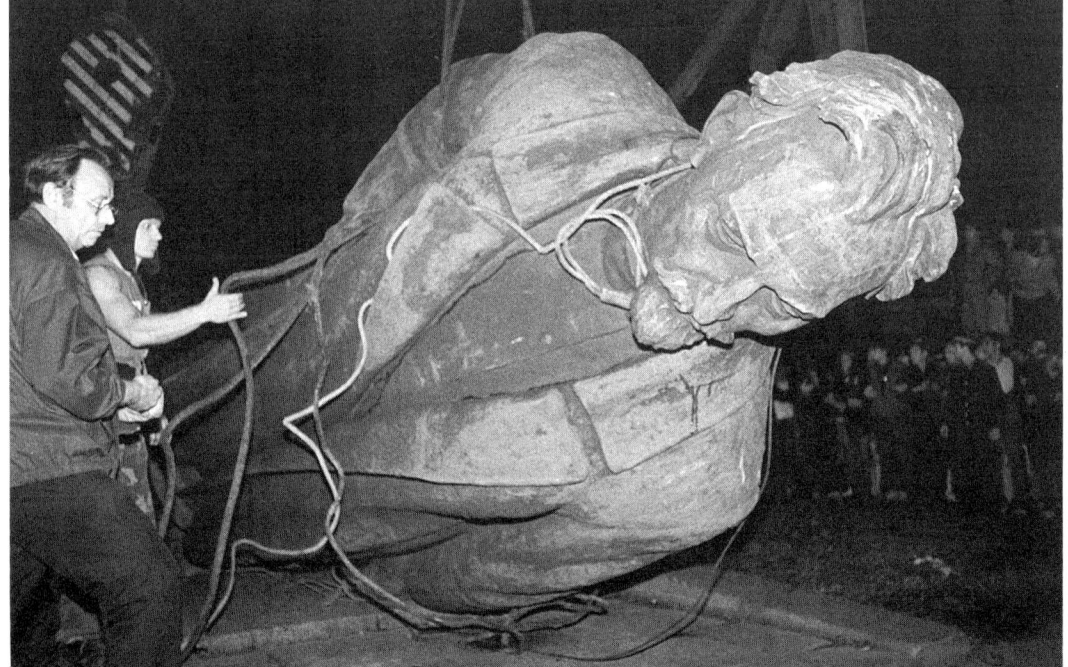

December, and Yeltsin found himself in the position of leader of the newly independent state of Russia. Nine of the republics of the former Soviet Union joined together with Russia and formed a far less cohesive confederation, the Commonwealth of Independent States.

Westerners have always found Yeltsin's popularity difficult to understand. During the late 1980s, when Gorbachev and Yeltsin clashed on many issues, westerners criticized Yeltsin's blunt, unpolished manner, favoring Gorbachev's suave, sophisticated style. Later, when Gorbachev fell from power, the European and American press still resisted Yeltsin, even though the Russian people so clearly loved him. Yeltsin's career as a statesman has been a series of struggles, in which his tough, dogged personality has helped him rise from a small Communist party bureaucrat to a position of world renown.

When news of the coup first shook the world, people feared that the years of Soviet reform and democratization would be canceled out, and the whole country would turn back to its dark days of repression and dictatorship. But one man's choice to defy the coup plotters, and to lead others to fight for what they believed in, changed the course of history. The coup functioned as a catalyst for Yeltsin, and he seized the opportunity and showed courage and determination in the face of guns and tanks. What might have been a return to the Dark Ages became instead a leap forward into a new democratic era in Russian politics.

Young Boris Nikolayevich Yeltsin poses with his parents, Klavdia Vasilievna and Nikolai Ignatievich. Yeltsin's parents were hardworking peasants who lived in the tiny village of Butko in northern Russia.

2

Fighting the Odds

BORIS NIKOLAYEVICH YELTSIN WAS BORN on February 1, 1931, in the village of Butko in the Ural Mountains of northern Russia. The Yeltsin family had inhabited this small village for many generations, farming the land and living a peasant life-style. All the farmers who lived in the region led a poor, harsh existence. Yeltsin's mother, Klavdia Vasilievna Starygin, and his father, Nikolai Ignatievich, were hardworking peasants who had been brought up in Butko. Boris, their first child, was later joined by a brother, Mikhail, and a sister, Valya. As a boy, Yeltsin was tall, and had thick brown hair and an athletic build. In his autobiography, *Against the Grain*, which was published in 1990, Yeltsin explains how difficult his childhood had been—there were bad harvests, a lack of food, and bands of outlaws that robbed and murdered at will without retribution. Yeltsin recalled how the family lived in near poverty, in a tiny house with one cow. His parents owned a horse, but when it died they had no animal to pull the plow.

A family of hungry peasants arrive in Moscow with their wagon of possessions in 1921. In his memoirs, Yeltsin recalled how his own family lived in near poverty when he was a child.

Yeltsin's family has a history of heartiness and longevity; his grandfathers and great-grandfathers lived past the age of 90, despite the hardships of Russian peasant life. From the very beginning of his life, Yeltsin was facing danger and surviving. In his autobiography, Yeltsin describes how he almost did not outlive his own baptism. At a small country church, the priest, who had been drinking toasts and baptizing babies all morning long, had become quite tipsy by the time the Yeltsin family brought their baby boy to him for baptizing. The baby was handed to the priest, who dropped him in the baptismal font. The priest was then distracted by someone in the congregation, and forgot to take the infant out of the holy water. When his mother realized what had transpired, she frantically pulled her child from the font and shook the water out of him. The priest, who seemed unconcerned, said, "Well, if he can survive such an ordeal it means he's a good tough lad . . . and I name him Boris [after a Russian martyr, Prince Boris]."

Even though the Bolsheviks (the political party headed by Vladimir Ilich Lenin, who led the revolution of 1917) had declared the Soviet Union an atheistic state after the 1917 revolution, the majority of peasants still practiced Orthodox Christianity, including the ritual of baptism. Therefore, it was not unusual for Yeltsin to be baptized in 1931; however, he never developed the same religious attitudes as his ancestors because his generation grew up in an environment that strongly discouraged belief in God and religion.

By 1931, the peasants of the Urals had been forced to give up farming for themselves and to join collective farms under the policy of collectivization begun by the Soviet leader Joseph Stalin. (Stalin ruled the Soviet Union as dictator from 1924 to 1953.) Collective farms were centralized farms where the state owned the land, and groups of farmers worked together on one large farm. Whole villages, where each peasant had farmed his or her own land, were dismantled and converted into large, collective farms. The food grown on collective farms was distributed by the government, and the farmers all received the same salary. During the 1930s, Stalin also created the policy of grain requisition. Under this program, peasants had to give all their grain to the state grain collectors for central distribution, and the peasants were senselessly left to starve. These policies of collectivization and grain requisition caused massive famine and death. Millions of peasants died throughout the Soviet Union during the 1930s and 1940s. Those who were able to survive did so by developing an ability to endure the harshest conditions and by working extremely hard.

The Yeltsin family worked on a collective farm, just like most of the peasants in the region, but in 1935, when the family cow died, Yeltsin's father and grandfather had to go from house to house looking for work. Yeltsin's father decided that in order to subsist, the whole family should leave the farm, and he and his father should look for work at a construction site.

In 1930, Soviet laborers sort and grade spring seeds in what was formerly a Russian church. Although Lenin declared the Soviet Union an atheistic state after the 1917 revolution, most Russian peasants continued to practice Orthodox Christianity.

A mass of peasants march to work on a collective farm, the New Life, in the Moscow district, circa 1930. The peasants of the Urals, including Yeltsin's parents, had been forced to give up their own farms and join centralized, state-owned farms under Stalin's policy of collectivization.

Stalin and his associates in the Kremlin developed a plan for the rapid industrialization of the entire Soviet Union. The Soviet leadership wanted to quickly transform the Soviet Union from an agricultural country, dominated by peasants who made up 90 percent of the population, to a highly advanced, industrial country with a population made up of proletarian workers. Those in power hoped that these grandiose plans would help the USSR become a superpower. They also hoped to show the rest of the world the superiority of the Communist system of government. The central government prepared a five-year plan for the industrialization of the country, and recruited millions of workers to build factories, roads, and bridges. The plan, however, turned out to be a utopian dream. It did not take into account the basic needs or rights of the people who were working to build up the country. Just as had happened in the course of the collectivization campaign, millions of people died during the rush to industrialize the Soviet Union. Accidents occurred constantly at the construction sites, and people froze or starved to death in the horrible living conditions. Although the exact number of victims in the collectivization and industrialization

On October 27, 1932, thousands of Russians attend the opening ceremony of the Dnieprostroi Dam. The dam, built by 25,000 laborers over a period of five years, was one of the many projects created during Stalin's industrialization campaign.

programs will probably never be known, some historians have estimated that 5 to 10 million peasants alone starved to death between 1928 and 1934.

Yeltsin's family, unable to survive on the collective farm, was forced to join the teeming masses that tried to endure the industrialization campaign. The family harnessed itself to a cart loaded with its few earthly possessions and walked 20 miles to the railway station to take a train to the town of Berezniki. There, Yeltsin's father found work in a new potash plant. (Potash is a compound that is used to make fertilizers, soap, and glass.) The job was grueling and dangerous, and Yeltsin's father had to carry heavy loads and breathe in clouds of dust daily. Millions of Stalin's proletarian workers eventually died performing the type of work Yeltsin's father had to do.

For the next 10 years, the six members of the family, Yeltsin, his parents, his brother and sister, and his grandfather, lived in one room of a wooden clapboard barracks with no plumbing or heat. The barracks hut had one central corridor with 20 small rooms adjoining it, and each room served as the living quarters for an entire family. The Yeltsins, including the family goat, all slept together in one room. In *Against the Grain*, Yeltsin remembers how hard their lives were then. He wrote that the winters were the worst because there was nowhere to hide from the biting cold. They had no warm clothes, so they huddled up to the goat for warmth. It was the goat, he said, that saved them during World War II (1939–45); even though the goat gave less than a liter of milk a day, it was enough to help the children survive.

Yeltsin had a peaceful and loving relationship with his mother. He describes her as "a gentle and kind woman by nature, [she] would help everyone by sewing clothes for all. . . . Every night she would sit down with her sewing, never taking money for her work. She was most grateful if someone gave her, say, half a loaf of bread or some other morsel of food."

Yeltsin's relationship with his father did not have the same harmonious quality. He describes his father as "rough and quick-tempered," traits he feels he has inherited. Whenever Yeltsin misbehaved, his father would beat him with a strap. Yeltsin recalls some of these violent punishments in his autobiography, and writes that they always occurred in silence, except for his mother's cries and pleas for his father not to touch him. Yeltsin's father would resolutely close the door, however, and while he told Yeltsin to lie down, his son would roll up his shirt and lower his pants. Throughout his beatings, Yeltsin always clenched his teeth, not making a sound, which incensed his father. Yeltsin's mother would always rush in, grab the strap away from her husband and push him aside, defending her son.

Despite the cramped and primitive conditions of the single rooms in which they lived, and the violent nature of Yeltsin's father, the families in the barracks tried to be neighborly and make the best of their miserable situation. Whenever they would celebrate a birthday or wedding, the whole barracks would wind up an old gramophone and play the three records they all shared. Day-to-day life remained difficult, however. Yeltsin said of this period of his life: "It was a fairly joyless time. There was never any question of sweets, delicacies or anything of that sort; we had only one aim in life—to survive."

The strain of living through the collectivization and the industrialization campaigns left Yeltsin with a feeling of hatred for Stalin and the cruelty he and his associates inflicted on the Soviet people. One particular incident that occurred one night in 1937 left a deep scar on Yeltsin's memory.

The late 1930s marked the height of Stalin's purges, when he tried to get rid of people he believed to be undesirables or rivals. At first, Stalin ordered government officials, who were suspected of treason or spying to be arrested. Soon, millions of innocent citizens found that they, too, could suddenly be arrested without warning. The majority of these victims never returned to their families. Sentences for the unwitting victims ranged from indefinite exile in a labor camp to execution by a firing squad. The most prominent victims were tried in "show trials" (fake trials where the accused were forced to sign confessions of guilt), but most ordinary citizens never received a hearing, and once they disappeared it became very difficult to learn of their fate. Stalin's paranoia went to horrific extremes. He not only had the majority of his associates murdered, but he also had innumerable generals and officers in the Red army killed just before the outbreak of World War II.

In 1937, when Yeltsin was six years old, his father was arrested in the middle of the night and taken away with no explanation. It is unclear how long the elder Yeltsin remained in police custody, but the police eventually released him and he returned to his family.

When Yeltsin started elementary school in Berezniki, he became a rowdy prankster, always devising schemes and playing practical jokes. As ringleader, he led the other children in devilish antics, and his bad behavior almost resulted in his expulsion from school on a number of occasions. One time, Yeltsin encouraged his whole fifth grade class to jump out of a first floor window, so when the teacher entered the classroom, she found it empty. The teacher finally discovered the whole class giggling outside, and she punished them all with a bad grade for behavior. Despite his rambunctious actions in school, Yeltsin always received top marks—fives on the Soviet five-point scale.

Sometimes Yeltsin's mischief was far more rough. He often engaged in gang wars, fighting with sticks or fists. Of one fight where someone knocked him over the head, he wrote:

> To this day I have a broken nose like a boxer's, from when someone caught me a whack with the shaft of a cart. I fell,

In 1936, during the height of Stalin's purges, workers take a vote for a resolution demanding severe punishment for "the enemies of the people." Millions of innocent citizens were arrested without warning, given so-called show trials, and sent to labor camps, or worse.

everything went black and I thought it was the end of me. But all was well; I came to my senses and was carried home. There were no fatalities in these fights, because although we fought enthusiastically, we still observed certain limits. It was more in the way of a sporting contest, though a very tough one.

The fights, the harsh living conditions, and Yeltsin's natural inclination to challenge authority all worked simultaneously to create a tough, courageous, and proud boy who often threw caution to the wind in favor of danger and adventure.

To help his parents, Yeltsin, seen here as a teenager, looked after his sister, Valya, whenever he could. By the age of 14, Yeltsin already showed great self-confidence and courage at school, where he publicly questioned the abilities of his homeroom teacher, whom he claimed abused her students.

3

The Young Rebel

YELTSIN'S BOISTEROUS BEHAVIOR in school finally led to his expulsion at the end of seventh grade. The incident that precipitated the expulsion occurred at the school graduation ceremony (primary school ended after the seventh grade) in an atmosphere of celebration and goodwill. As usual, Yeltsin refused to be cooperative, despite the dignified occasion. After asking permission to speak, Yeltsin stood up in the middle of the ceremony and said a few hasty words of thanks to most of his teachers. Then he lashed out at the woman who had been his homeroom teacher for seven years. He announced that this woman had no right to teach and that she "crippled" her students. He described how the teacher abused her students by hitting them and making them do chores for her at her home. Yeltsin later wrote about this incident at the school graduation ceremony: "Briefly, at that solemn gathering I described how she used to mock her pupils, destroy their self-confidence and do everything possible to humiliate every one of us. ...There was an uproar. The whole event was ruined."

The next day the school principal informed Yeltsin that he would not be permitted to attend secondary school (high school) anywhere in the USSR. When Yeltsin's father heard about the incident, he tried to punish his son with a beating, but Yeltsin grabbed his father's arm and shouted, "That's enough! From now on I'm going to educate myself."

Yeltsin refused to accept the school staff's decision to terminate his schooling. He took his case to every education official he could find, eventually pleading it to the local Communist party committee. A commission to investigate Yeltsin's case concluded that the teacher in question was indeed unfit to teach, and it dismissed her. The commission also restored Yeltsin's certificate, allowing him to enter high school. Yeltsin vindicated himself, and although he had to struggle to prove his point, in the end he won the battle. Yeltsin's courage and indignation at injustice had already become apparent at the young age of 14.

During his years in school, Yeltsin developed a love of sports. After participating in such sports as skiing, gymnastics, boxing, and wrestling, he found that he had a special talent for volleyball. Yeltsin went to extremes in his devotion to the game. He even placed a volleyball beside his pillow at night so that as soon as he woke up in the morning he could train by himself. He never wanted to stop playing. Participation in a team sport demanded discipline, a penchant for hard work, and drive—qualities that Yeltsin strove to achieve. Years later, when Yeltsin attended the Urals Polytechnic Institute (equivalent to an American college) in Sverdlovsk, he took volleyball even more seriously. Yeltsin believed in devoting himself fully to his academic work and to sports, but these activities left him with virtually no free time, even for sleep. In his autobiography, he writes that volleyball had been a significant part of his life. In college, playing volleyball and instructing four teams absorbed about six hours of his day, and Yeltsin discovered that he was only able to study late at night. Furthermore, he had trained himself to go without much sleep, resting only about four hours each night.

But catching a volleyball became more difficult after Yeltsin lost two of his fingers in a dangerous prank during World War II. He and some friends had decided to look for some grenades, in order to take them apart and figure out how they worked. Always the ringleader, Yeltsin stole a grenade from a church that functioned as an ammunition storehouse, and together with his friends, crept into the forest at night to perform the experiment. Yeltsin told the other boys to take cover while, unaware of the consequences, he took a hammer and smashed the grenade. The grenade exploded and two of Yeltsin's fingers on his left hand were blown up. The other boys, who were unharmed, carried the wounded Yeltsin back to town. By this time, gangrene had infected Yeltsin's hand, and he had to have the two fingers amputated. In time, Yeltsin developed his own method of catching the volleyball, albeit not the standard method. It was, however, just as efficient.

Yeltsin had a tendency toward putting himself and his friends in life-threatening situations. One summer, after ninth grade, Yeltsin led a few other boys in an expedition through the taiga (a subarctic evergreen forest much like the Alaskan wilderness) of the Urals. The boys went in search of the source of the Yaiva River. After hiking and camping out for a few days, the boys ran out of food and had to live on nuts, mushrooms, berries, and whatever else they could find in the forest to eat. Eventually, they found the source of the river, which was a spring of natural hydrogen sulfide.

Delighted with their discovery, the boys turned back to begin their trip home through the dense and uninhabited wilderness. By the time they came upon a village, the trek had exhausted them, and they decided to obtain a boat so they could float down the river the rest of the way home. After finding a peasant who was willing to barter with them, the boys gathered together all of their belongings of any worth—a knapsack, a knife, and a belt—and traded them for a small wooden rowboat. As they floated downstream, the boys enjoyed the pristine landscape.

Lying around, however, had never been a part of Yeltsin's nature, and as soon as he spotted an interesting cave in a hillside, he persuaded the others to explore it with him. After climbing through the cave, they came out on the other side of the hill, finding themselves deep in the taiga, and they realized they had lost their way. They could not find the river or the boat and wandered through the wilderness for a week. This particular region of the taiga was swampy, and they could not find fresh water to drink. In desperation to quench their thirst, they drank the dirty swamp water.

Finally, after days of searching, they found their boat and collapsed into it. By then they had all contracted typhoid fever from drinking the infested swamp water, and their body temperatures had risen to 103 degrees. Delirious with fever, the boys drifted downstream, losing consciousness off and on. Somehow Yeltsin forced himself to tie the boat to a bridge, hoping that someone would find them. When they finally were rescued, they discovered they had been lost for a month and had missed the first month of school. The boys were taken to a hospital where they remained sick with typhoid for almost three months.

The illness set all of the boys except Yeltsin back a year in school. This being his tenth and final year of school, Yeltsin refused to be held back, and he began to study at home for the final exams as soon as he recovered from his illness. But when he went to school to take the exams, the teachers informed him that he could not because he had not attended school. Yeltsin would not accept this decision. He fought the bureaucracy by appealing his case to the local education department and Communist party committee, and his excellent record as a volleyball player helped him gain admittance to the exams, which he passed.

After high school, Yeltsin decided to study civil engineering, perhaps because of his father's work in the construction business. Yeltsin's grandfather, a stubborn man, felt that before Yeltsin could begin his course work at the Urals Polytechnic Institute, he had to perform one more test to prove himself. In *Against the Grain* Yeltsin described the challenge his 70-year-old grandfather set before him. His grandfather told him that he could not enter the building trade until he had built something with his own hands. He told Yeltsin to build him a bathhouse and to construct the walls and roof by himself—including cutting down the pine trees, preparing the moss caulking for the walls, and carrying the logs two miles to the building site. He even told Yeltsin that he must make the foundations and do the joinery himself. His grandfather did not come anywhere near Yeltsin while he was working, nor did he help him at all, even when Yeltsin had to raise the roof beams. Yeltsin passed his grandfather's test of strength and manhood, and entered the Urals Polytechnic Institute in the fall of 1949.

After his first year at school, Yeltsin became restless to see more of the USSR. He did not have a kopeck (equivalent to a penny) with which to travel, so he became a hobo for the summer, hitchhiking on trucks and trains. Numerous times the police stopped Yeltsin and asked him where he was going. Yeltsin wrote of these incidents, "I would say I was going to see my grandmother in, for instance, Simferopol in the Crimea. 'In which street does she live?' Since I knew that every Soviet town has a Lenin Street, I was never wrong in giving that as my grandmother's address and they would let me go."

By the time Yeltsin returned home after two months of being a hobo, his clothes were in tatters, his shoes had no soles, and he had lost his watch and his extra set of clothes in a card game to a bunch of ex-convicts.

When Yeltsin returned to the Urals Polytechnic Institute, he continued to receive excellent grades and to play

Yeltsin coached a women's volleyball team while he was a student at the Urals Polytechnic Institute in Sverdlovsk. He was an excellent volleyball player in spite of a childhood injury in which he lost the thumb and forefinger of his left hand.

his beloved volleyball, but he overexerted himself by training too much. At one point, he fell ill with quinsy, a severe inflammation of the throat accompanied by a high fever. He collapsed on the court, and had to be taken to a hospital. The doctors warned Yeltsin that he had to stay in bed for a minimum of four months or he would develop heart disease. Despite the risk to his life, Yeltsin did not heed these warnings, and after a few days he escaped from the hospital by lowering himself from a window with the help of his friends.

Yeltsin stole away to his parents' home in Berezniki, where he rested. After a few days he tried to play volleyball again. At first his heart would pound wildly and he could only last for a minute or two, but he persisted, and after a month he could play a whole game again. When he returned to the Institute in Sverdlovsk (today called Yekaterinburg), a doctor examined him and told him that he had been very lucky that his heart had recovered with no damage, despite the risks he had taken.

Yeltsin and his classmates at the Institute grew to be very close friends during their years together, and when their studies came to an end in 1955 they all made a pact to meet every five years and spend their summer vacation together. They have kept that pact, and every five years they gather together to go camping out in the wilderness or sailing down one of Russia's many rivers.

In 1955, when Yeltsin graduated from the Institute, he received his first job assignment as a foreman on a construction site. Under the Communist system, employment was guaranteed to all graduates of universities and institutes, and to all people of working age. Candidates did not interview for a variety of jobs, but had to take whatever job the state assigned to them. Once again, Yeltsin bucked the system by refusing his first job assignment. He decided that he still needed on-the-job training. Yeltsin later explained his decision to reject the foreman job in *Against the Grain*, where he states his belief that it would have been a mistake to supervise construction workers when he had never had the experience of performing such work himself. He also realized that as team leader he would be at a disadvantage because his workers would have more practical knowledge of the work than he had.

Yeltsin resolved to spend one year learning the 12 basic trades in construction work. He spent one month studying each trade, including how to lay bricks, make and pour concrete, carpenter, drive trucks, glaze, plaster, and paint. Only at the end of his year of practical, "real life" training would Yeltsin take a job as foreman on a construction site. At first Yeltsin found his job relatively easy, but he soon encountered unexpected complications that tested his wits and managerial capabilities. Sometimes groups of convicts were assigned to work under Yeltsin's management. The convicts intimidated most foremen into paying higher wages than the average rate. Yeltsin decided not to pay the convicts any more than the other workers earned. On pay day, Yeltsin almost paid with his life for his resolution not to give in to the convicts' demands. He related this tense situation in his autobiography:

> Soon a hulking giant of a man came into my little foreman's office, carrying an axe which he raised and held over me saying, "Are you going to pay us at the proper rate like they always paid us before you came along, you puppy?" I said, "No." "In that case," he countered, "just you remember that I've got nothing to lose. I'll smash your skull before you've even had time to squeak." I could see from the look in his eyes that he might easily split my head open without batting an eyelid.
>
> I could have dodged him, of course, or tried somehow to tackle him physically, although it was a cramped little room and the axe was already poised over my head. So I decided on an unexpected move. I have a very loud, powerful voice, and, with great effect in that tiny room, I gave a sharp, full-throated roar of "Get out," while looking him straight in the eye. He suddenly lowered his axe, dropped it, turned around and went out in silence, his back bent in submission.

Yeltsin distinguished himself as a highly competent and skilled construction engineer while working as a foreman. Gradually, he moved up the ranks, eventually becoming the chief engineer and general manager of a construction enterprise (factory) that made prefabricated apartments. Yeltsin's new position put him in charge of 20,000 people, and he continued to impose his rigorous standards on his huge work force. He once characterized his style of work as "tough." He expected his people to behave correctly and to keep their word after they gave it. Yeltsin never swore and tried not to raise his thunderous, piercing voice at people. He said that the chief weapons in the battle for discipline were his own complete dedication to the job, a constant insistence on high standards, and the continual checking of work. He also said that just as a person's good work never went unrecognized, bad work did not go unnoticed either. "If you've given your word," he declared in *Against the Grain*, "keep it, and if you don't keep it—you must answer for it." Yeltsin's fair and comprehensible attitudes established an environment of mutual confidence between managers and workers.

In a moment of relaxation, Yeltsin (standing, far left) clowns around with some school friends from the Polytechnic Institute.

By 1961, Yeltsin distinguished himself as a highly skilled construction engineer and became the general manager of a factory that made prefabricated housing similar to the apartment building shown here.

In 1961, at the young age of 30, Yeltsin received the post of general manager of the large industrial complex. By this time, he had married Anastasia (Naya) Girina, whom he had met while he was a student at the Urals Polytechnic Institute. Naya was enrolled in the engineering program. Yeltsin and Naya immediately became close friends when they met, but the relationship remained platonic until their second year, when Yeltsin kissed Naya behind a pillar at the Institute. After graduation, Yeltsin received his assignment to stay on in Sverdlovsk, but Naya had to go to Orenburg, a town far from Sverdlovsk. The couple decided to test their love for each other, and a year later they met in Kuibyshev, a town between Orenburg and Sverdlovsk. As soon as they saw each other they knew they would spend the rest of their lives together, and they married in 1956. Yeltsin wrote of his love for his wife:

> The whole of my subsequent life has proved that we were brought together by fate. It was one of those one-in-a-thousand choices. Naya took me and loved me as I am—obstinate and prickly—and naturally she has not had an easy time with me. As for myself, I need hardly say that I have always loved her—gentle, tender and kind as she is—and will love her all my life.

In 1957, they had their first daughter, Lena, and two years later their second daughter, Tanya, was born.

Up to this point in his life, Yeltsin had no interest in political affairs. He had carved out a solid, respectable job for himself in construction engineering. Years later, when Yeltsin immersed himself in politics, he valued his years in the construction industry and never forgot what he had learned while working with manual laborers. Yeltsin's peasant origins, his tough personality, and his work in construction gave him credibility with the Russian people.

Throughout his life, Yeltsin has taken many risks to fight injustice. By the time he became a politician in Moscow in 1985, he had survived car accidents, a plane crash, and an attempt on his life. With characteristic good humor he looked back on all these incidents saying, "I must have more lives than all the Moscow cats put together."

This portrait of Yeltsin was taken while he served as an alternate (non-voting) member of the Politburo of the Communist Party of the Soviet Union's Central Committee (CPSU). Before the August 1991 coup attempt, the Politburo was an elite body of 20 members, who were elected from and by the Central Committee, and was the center of executive power in the Soviet Union.

4

A Member of the Party

YELTSIN JOINED the Communist Party of the Soviet Union (CPSU) in 1961, the same year that he became head of the construction complex. At that point, becoming a member of the party could be seen as a natural progression in Yeltsin's career. He had achieved a high managerial position, and now he needed to join the Soviet elite—the people who actually dictated the course of the economic system. Yeltsin joined the CPSU out of a genuine conviction that communism represented a just and fair ideology. He wrote in his autobiography, "I believed sincerely in the ideals of justice which the party espoused; with equal sincerity I joined the party, having carefully studied the party statute, the program and the classics, re-read Lenin, Marx and Engels. It is only recently that we have begun considering the negative role played by the party's interference in economic affairs."

In 1961, Nikita Khrushchev, the leader of the Soviet Union, had instituted a policy that came to be known as the thaw (as in melting ice). Stalin had died in 1953, and with his death, the era of dictatorship in the Soviet Union came to an end. Stalin had led the Soviet Union since 1924, the year that Lenin, the first leader of the Soviet Union, had died. A power struggle ensued after Stalin's death, but by 1956, Khrushchev had ascended to the top position in the country. Slowly, Khrushchev started to make amends for the horrors that had occurred under Stalin. In February 1956, at the 20th Party Congress, Khrushchev denounced Stalin in what was supposed to be a secret speech to a closed cabinet of the political elite. Someone, however, leaked the speech to a reporter from the West, and soon the whole world began to comprehend the extent of Stalin's crimes. The Soviet Union was a highly secretive and repressive totalitarian state, especially under Stalin, and Khrushchev's speech marked the first revelations of Stalin's purges, the cruel and murderous treatment of the peasantry under collectivization, and the human costs of the industrialization campaign. It had been unthinkable, even suicidal, to criticize Stalin while he was alive, but after his death Khrushchev felt compelled to admit the terrors that had occurred under his leadership in order to begin to heal the country.

In addition to revealing Stalin's crimes, Khrushchev instituted a liberalization policy (a precursor of Gorbachev's policy of glasnost), under which censorship became less severe, formerly banned books could be published in the country, artists were allowed to use more abstract expressions in their work (under Stalin, an artist's work had to conform to a style called socialist realism, the optimistic portrayal of socialist society in conventionally realistic terms), and many of the victims of the purges who had survived the labor camps were allowed to return home. Soviet culture flourished briefly during the thaw, but by 1964, Khrushchev had been secretly ousted from power by his competitors and conservative opponents in the Kremlin.

Under the next leader, Leonid Brezhnev, who had joined the plot to remove Khrushchev, the liberalism of the thaw ended and a long period of cultural and political repression followed. The Brezhnev regime's stance on foreign policy perpetuated the idea of promoting communism around the world. During the Brezhnev years, the Soviet army first invaded Czechoslovakia in 1968 and then Afghanistan in 1979. Although Brezhnev helped develop the concept of détente, or peaceful coexistence with the West, the cold war continued throughout his time in office. (The cold war between the United States and the Soviet Union, which lasted for 40 years, from the early 1950s to the late 1980s, was a conflict over ideological differences between the two adversaries—fought not with weapons, but with power politics, economic pressure, espionage, and hostile propaganda.) Brezhnev died in 1982, having held power for 18 years. During his tenure, Brezhnev had not ruled as a dictator, as Stalin had, but instead had shared

On January 1, 1980, Afghan students demonstrate against Soviet intervention in Afghanistan as they display a banner that reads: "Afghanistan is Vi[e]tnam of USSR." Under Soviet leader Leonid Brezhnev, Soviet troops invaded Afghanistan on December 27, 1979, to help prop up its pro-Soviet regime.

power with a few close associates, creating an oligarchy (government by the few). His style of sharing power, and for many years acting only as a figurehead, allowed him to stay in office until his death at the age of 76.

After Brezhnev's death, Yuri Andropov led the Soviet Union briefly, until he died in 1984. Konstantin Chernenko, another aging bureaucrat, became the next Soviet leader, but he, too, was ill; he died a year later, paving the way for Gorbachev's ascension to power in 1985.

Not until Mikhail Gorbachev became head of the country did the idea of a liberalization of society come alive again. At first, Gorbachev began with reforms similar to those enacted under Khrushchev, but soon the glasnost reforms took on a momentum of their own and had a much more liberating effect than those that were implemented during Khrushchev's thaw.

A composite of photographs displays the eight men who led the Soviet Union from 1917 to 1991. Beginning at the top, from left to right, are Lenin, Stalin, Khrushchev, and Brezhnev; at the bottom are Kosygin, Andropov, Chernenko, and Gorbachev.

Yeltsin's career moved forward rapidly after he joined the Communist party, and it increasingly took on a more political bent. In 1969, he received an offer to become the senior head of the Communist party section responsible for all construction in the province of Sverdlovsk. Yeltsin accepted the new job with little enthusiasm because it meant giving up his hands-on involvement in the construction industry for a purely political assignment. He had worked in the construction industry for 14 years, and he liked his work. Yeltsin wrote, however, that he took the political job because he wanted to move in a new direction, and he soon discovered that he excelled in politics.

In 1976, Yeltsin was summoned to Moscow to meet with Brezhnev, who appointed him first secretary of Sverdlovsk's Communist party. A Western reporter later wrote of Yeltsin's rise in the party ranks, "It was an exeptionally fast promotion for someone with only fifteen years in the party." Yeltsin remained in the position of Sverdlovsk first secretary for nine years, and gained approval and support both from Moscow and the local leadership.

Many scholars have wondered how an outspoken rebel such as Yeltsin could have gained so much popularity with the people in Sverdlovsk and in the conservative, conformist administration of the Brezhnev era. Even Yeltsin himself questioned how he got caught up in the political maelstrom of the time:

> I sometimes wonder how I managed to land up among all these people. Why was it that a system, perfected over the years and specifically designed to select only people of a certain type, should have suddenly failed so badly as to choose Yeltsin? Admittedly I didn't last long among them, and I bolted like a caged animal when I could stand it no longer, but this had never happened over seven decades.

One explanation for Yeltsin's success and popularity is that during the Brezhnev years, the central leadership left Yeltsin on his own and he flourished with so much independence. Another reason for Yeltsin's popularity given

As first secretary of the Communist party of Sverdlovsk Province, Yeltsin assists in the harvesting of potatoes. Leonid Brezhnev appointed Yeltsin first secretary in 1976 despite Yeltsin's having served only 15 years in the CPSU.

by an observer of Soviet affairs is that, "Under Brezhnev's policy of 'stability of cadres,' provincial party first secretaries could be virtually sure of keeping their jobs for life, unless their level of incompetence or corruption became outrageous." John Morrison, who wrote *Boris Yeltsin: From Bolshevik to Democrat* (1991), believes another possible reason for Yeltsin's popularity is his ability to get results. Morrison explains, "In a system without real economic incentives it was only the drive and initiative of the party first secretary that determined whether milk appeared in the shops, housing was built on schedule, and factories fulfilled their plans. If they did, the first secretary was left in peace."

When Gorbachev instituted his policy of glasnost, one of his main motivations was a desire to revitalize Soviet society. During the previous administrations, the totalitarian nature of the government had suppressed free speech, silenced religious organizations, and prohibited people from gathering for any kind of private club or meeting. A primary goal of glasnost and perestroika was to create a civil society in the Soviet Union, independent of the state's jurisdiction. Under Brezhnev, society had begun to stagnate. The economy swirled downward, and corruption in business, politics, and social services turned the Soviet Union into a country on the verge of collapse.

Although Yeltsin himself steered clear of wrongdoing during the Brezhnev era, he repeatedly witnessed corruption in business and party dealings. He also encountered a high level of laziness and absenteeism. On numerous occasions buildings had to be completely reconstructed because of sloppy workmanship. The Soviet command economy, in which Gosplan, the central state planning commission, controlled and administered everything—including salaries—left no room for individual initiative. The state guaranteed all jobs, housing, education, health care, and child care. Individuals, however, had few personal rights. Most people were not allowed to move out of the city or the town in which they were born. Even visiting another city involved an enormous amount of paperwork to obtain permission and an internal passport (which is similar to an international passport but was for use only within the Soviet Union; it also functioned as an identification card). Peasants living on collective farms could not even visit other towns or cities because the state would not issue internal passports to them. (Gorbachev abolished this law when he took office in 1985.)

In the Soviet Union only one political party existed: the Communist party. The totalitarian system did not permit any other political party to form. Nor did it allow people to travel freely within the Soviet Union or internationally. The KGB decided who could leave the country, and there was a maximum quota of people per year allowed to travel outside Soviet borders.

When the Bolsheviks came to power in 1917, they envisioned a society where everyone—men and women—would have equal pay, equal rights, and an equal standard of living. They set to work centralizing the control of the economy and trying to create a utopian, classless society. Nevertheless, the Soviet Union soon became highly stratified, with a new elite that gained its status not from money, as the upper classes do in capitalist societies, but from power within the Communist party. By the time Yeltsin joined the Communist party in 1961, Soviet society had become one of "haves" and "have nots," like that of many capitalist countries. The "haves" included an elite of party members who wielded enough political influence to acquire the material comforts they desired. The "have nots" included lower level party members who did not have the right connections, and the majority of the population—nonparty members who made up the masses of poor workers. The party functioned as a mechanism for segregating society. Becoming a party member required years of hard work and a clean record, and even then one's acceptance was not guaranteed.

Another factor in the separation of Soviet society was individual nationality. Soviet society—Russian society in particular—was highly anti-Semitic, racist, and nationalistic. These biases came to be known as Russian chauvinism. In the other republics, such as Georgia and Armenia, reverse discrimination often occurred because people resented the dominant Russian and Soviet cultures that were imposed upon them from Moscow. From the beginning of Soviet rule, the national language of the USSR had been Russian, and all school children had to learn Russian before they learned their native language. (There are more than 100 nationalities and different languages spoken in the republics that made up the former Soviet Union.)

Working in the Communist party in Sverdlovsk, Yeltsin became very disillusioned with the Soviet system and with its solutions to the problems he witnessed daily. Yeltsin found himself trapped in a system he wanted to change, and he found he often had to fight for these changes alone. The Soviet system seemed to have worked relatively well in the past, and it was only gradually that Yeltsin came to realize that it would collapse unless its leaders undertook major reforms. In *Against the Grain*, Yeltsin describes his years working within the Soviet hierarchy:

> I was brought up in the system; everything was steeped in the methods of the "command" system and I, too, acted accordingly. Whether I was chairing a meeting, running

my office, or delivering a report to a plenum—everything that one did was expressed in terms of pressure, threats and coercion. At the time these methods did produce some results, especially if the boss in question was sufficiently strong-willed. Gradually, though, one became more and more aware that what had seemed to be reliable and correct instructions by the party bureau turned out, on checking, not to have been done at all.... The system was clearly beginning to fail.

During the cold war, the Soviet leadership's propaganda encouraged the Soviet people to believe that their standard of living equaled or surpassed that of people living in the

In September 1989, tens of thousands of Azeri nationalists defy Kremlin warnings and gather near a giant statue of Lenin in the main square in Baku, Azerbaijan, prior to President Gorbachev's announcement of major reforms, including his policies of glasnost and perestroika.

West. Within the USSR, the elite—the privileged who had access to better food, doctors, clothes, homes, and cars—perpetuated these falsehoods. When the Soviet Union began to crumble, those who had benefited from the corruption and privileges of the Communist party fought tooth and nail to preserve the status quo.

In fact, the standard of living for the majority of the Soviet people was far below that of most people in Western Europe and the United States. Even today, few people in the former Soviet Union own cars, washing machines, dryers, dishwashers, and other electrical appliances. These are luxuries enjoyed only by the upper crust of society. Special stores, hospitals, hotels, theaters, and vacation areas were reserved for top party members, and these privileges created a pyramidlike system in which one tiny part of society lived like kings while the majority lived like paupers. A black market thrived alongside the state-owned stores, where many shelves were bare. Everyone had to trade in the black market on one level or another, simply to survive.

One of the foremost ideological premises of communism is the idea that there is no private property. Ideally, under communism, everything is to be owned communally, or as in the Soviet case, owned by the state. For all their privileges, the Soviet elite never owned any of their luxuries. The cars, dachas, and resorts were all owned by the state. One could gain access to these benefits, but just as quickly, one could lose them. All it took was a political mistake or a forced retirement.

The pyramid system reached its height under Stalin, who enjoyed his position at the top, where he pulled all the strings. Yeltsin describes the system bitterly in his memoirs, and explains that the individual owned nothing under Stalin. As a dictator, Stalin controlled everyone. His terror extended so far that he even imprisoned the wives of his own advisers, Mikhail Kalinin and Vyacheslav

Molotov, and neither man dared to speak out to save his wife for fear of being executed himself.

Things changed dramatically after Stalin's death in 1953, but some of the fundamentals of the system remained in place right until the Soviet Union dissolved. The more entrenched Yeltsin became in his party job, the more he found himself caught up in the party system, with all of its corruption and elitism. In 1985, when he became a member of the Politburo (an elite advisory panel that counseled the general secretary), an incident occurred that epitomized the cynical, absurd nature of the system. Yeltsin's chief bodyguard warned Yeltsin's wife and children not to feed him fruits or vegetables bought in the local market because they might be poisoned. When his daughter asked if the rest of the family could eat this produce, the bodyguard said that it would be all right. Yeltsin wrote resentfully of this incident, "In other words, you can go ahead and be poisoned, but he is sacred."

Yeltsin's reaction to the nepotism (favoritism shown to relatives) and corruption of the upper echelons of the party upset many bureaucrats within the system. They could not understand why he rejected a system that offered him a fancy dacha, high quality medicine, and other privileges. Yeltsin bucked the system by refusing the party's perks, and he worked to make changes that would bring about more equality in Russian society. In the end, Yeltsin's actions convinced the ordinary masses to trust him because they showed he clearly wanted to destroy elitism and injustice.

When Yeltsin was offered the advantages of a high-ranking party member, he said he could not accept them while others suffered around him. The Kremlin leaders had never encountered such a rebellious party member, and they soon tried to reverse the course of history by rejecting him. But it was too late. Soon the old guard would be swept away by this man who had become a thorn in its side.

On December 19, 1990, Yeltsin addresses the Congress of People's Deputies as his adversary President Gorbachev, seated behind him, listens.

5

The Rivals: Gorbachev and Yeltsin

MIKHAIL GORBACHEV, Yeltsin's principal political rival, was born only four weeks after Yeltsin in the small town of Privolnoye in Stavropol province in the fertile North Caucasus Mountains of southern Russia. Both men came from peasant families, but Yeltsin's family experienced poorer and harsher conditions. The pivotal difference between the two men centers on their involvement in the Communist party. Gorbachev's grandparents were party members, both his parents joined the party early on, and Gorbachev himself joined the party in 1952. These early ties to the party made Gorbachev far more reluctant to abandon Socialist ideals than Yeltsin, who had no family ties with the party. In comparing the two men, reporter John Morrison wrote in *Boris Yeltsin: From Bolshevik to Democrat*:

> The strength of the "red" family tradition emerged later as a crucial element in Gorbachev's value system, buttressing his deep personal

loyalty to communist ideals. As he told a group of writers and cultural figures in November 1990, he would never accept the idea of private land ownership or abandon the ideal of socialism because it would mean betraying the memory of his grandfather. Yeltsin's family appears to have had no such links to the Party, so perhaps his identification with it was never as deep as that of Gorbachev.

With their schooling, the two men's lives continued to diverge. Gorbachev, partly because of his consistent work with the CPSU, attended the highly prestigious Moscow

Cheering Communist youths carry a giant portrait of Joseph Stalin in the 1940s. Gorbachev had strong family ties with the Communist party and spent his early years in activities involving the Komsomol, or youth league. Yeltsin, on the other hand, never seemed to show a fervent interest in the party until he became a member at the age of 30.

State University, where he studied law, a far more political subject than construction engineering. While Yeltsin played volleyball, Gorbachev spent his time in activities connected with the Komsomol (the Communist party's youth league, similar to the Boy and Girl Scouts organizations in the United States). Gorbachev became a party member at the age of 21, whereas Yeltsin did not join the party until he was 30. Yeltsin also never seemed to have a passionate interest in the party, whereas Gorbachev's activities indicate a strong interest from an early age.

After graduating from their respective universities, Gorbachev pursued party work by returning to his native Stavropol to work as a Komsomol propagandist; Yeltsin, on the other hand, went to work in construction. In 1961, the year Yeltsin joined the party, Gorbachev attended the 22nd Party Congress in Moscow and heard a speech in which Khrushchev elaborated on the terrors that had occurred under Stalin.

By 1976, when Yeltsin became Sverdlovsk first secretary, Gorbachev had an equivalent post in the province of Stavropol. Even though they held similar posts, however, their backgrounds diverged tremendously—a factor that has indirectly affected their different attitudes towards the party and their contrasting leadership styles. Gorbachev had far more experience working within the Communist party when he began serving in Moscow in 1979, whereas Yeltsin only became involved in politics in his late thirties. Morrison commented on Yeltsin's lack of experience in politics:

> Interviewed in 1990 about his party background, Yeltsin said, "I am neither an official nor an apparatchik. I started as a worker and worked my way up step by step . . . I understand the people and the common man." Gorbachev, by contrast, never managed a farm, a factory, or a construction site, specializing instead in party organization, agitation, and propaganda. Unlike Yeltsin, he was a persuasive talker with considerable charm.

When Gorbachev became general secretary of the Communist party (the highest post in the Soviet government and equivalent to the presidency of the United States) in 1985, he offered Yeltsin a job in Moscow. Yeltsin and Gorbachev knew each other from their days as provincial party bosses, when they had called one another to barter for goods, exchanging, for example, metal and timber from Sverdlovsk for beef and poultry from Stavropol. Although Yeltsin had already had a few offers to move to Moscow, he had refused them all. When Gorbachev made his proposal, Yeltsin could no longer refuse. In 1985, after he received two phone calls from party members trying to persuade him to come to Moscow (one from Yeltsin's future nemesis Yegor Ligachev, a party conservative), Yeltsin moved reluctantly to the center of Soviet power.

Soon after his arrival in Moscow, Yeltsin received another promotion, this time to the influential position of head of the Moscow city committee of the Communist party (similar to the position of mayor in the United States). Out of 9 million inhabitants, the city committee had 1.2 million party members. Yeltsin's new position allowed him to become a nonvoting candidate member of the Politburo and would be present at all Politburo meetings.

Years later, looking back on his rapid move upward in the party, Yeltsin puzzled over why Gorbachev had picked him. In his autobiography, Yeltsin explains that he thought Gorbachev selected him because the Soviet leader understood his character and was sure that Yeltsin would be able to clean house—to fight the mafia and to eliminate the deadwood in personnel. Yeltsin had few illusions, however, and understood that his new appointment was also a political maneuver to unseat the current Moscow party chief, Viktor Grishin. Yeltsin recalls, "I agreed to accept the post, but with misgivings—not because I was afraid of the difficulties ahead, but because I fully realized that I was being used as the means of levering Grishin out of the job." Yeltsin did not have a high opinion of Grishin, whom he thought of as a scheming, untrustworthy bureaucrat, but he also did not like being used as a political tool. Gorbachev wanted to make sure he had no competitors for the position of general secretary, and he thought that Yeltsin's appointment and the removal of Grishin guaranteed his dominance.

Yeltsin's first act as Moscow party chief involved a purging of all of Grishin's former staff, holdovers from the pre-Gorbachev regime. Yeltsin's characteristic aggressive

Yeltsin visits a food store to talk with its workers. When he first arrived in Moscow, Yeltsin tried to purge the party of corruption and incompetence. He regularly visited local workers and shops to discuss various reforms and solicit the workers' advice about making additional improvements.

style and his wholesale dismissal of the staff ruffled many conservatives' feathers. In addition to firing personnel, Yeltsin brought his belief in the rejection of privileges and elitism to a city that epitomized the hierarchical nature of the Soviet system. From the beginning, Yeltsin visited factories and stores; he waited in line to buy food and to ride buses; and he took the metro (subway) regularly. Occasionally, he let the press know about his plans to visit local workers or shops, and he urged reporters to describe the corruption and inefficiency that he had uncovered. In his first year in Moscow, Yeltsin found that 35 percent of the city's buses sat idle every day, 65,000 children were waiting to be placed in a kindergarten, and 16 percent of the city's inhabitants still lived in communal apartments.

Yeltsin also discovered that people protected one another, and that they were too frightened to admit that thievery and corruption surrounded them. Occasionally, someone might reveal the truth about some negative aspect of the system to Yeltsin, but this was rare. Yeltsin recalled one such incident in which the informant was a frightened young woman. She recounted how she and all her coworkers had been forced to overcharge their customers and then pay the surplus to their supervisors. Almost every retail store in the city operated with this kind of kickback system. In his first year, Yeltsin helped to have approximately 800 people arrested, tried, and convicted for criminal offenses. But these arrests were only the tip of the iceberg. Yeltsin recalls his frustration, "We were never able to get our hands on the really big operators in the 'black economy' . . . neither could we touch the top end of the mafia, with its links to politicians."

When Yeltsin moved to Moscow, it was a hotbed of political controversy, for he went there during the time that Gorbachev introduced his policies of glasnost and perestroika. Yeltsin took the reform plans seriously and worked to implement them. Often he went much further in carrying out the reforms than any other politician was willing to go. In 1986, at the 27th Party Congress, Yeltsin gave a speech criticizing the party elite and the corruption he had witnessed in his first year in Moscow. Morrison later commented on Yeltsin's address, writing that it "was one of the most vigorous pleas for reform yet heard, going further than Gorbachev in denouncing what he called 'an inert layer of time-servers with party cards.'" Morrison also stated that in his speech, Yeltsin assailed the same people in the Central Committee apparatus whom he needed as allies if he had any aspiration to succeed in Moscow. Yeltsin then made a personal confession that recalled Nikita Khrushchev's so-called secret speech denouncing Stalin at the 20th Party Congress in 1956, in which he admitted his negligence in resisting Stalin. Imitating Khrushchev, Yeltsin asked, "Why did I not say this in my speech at the Twenty-sixth Party Congress [in 1981]? So be it. I can answer, and answer frankly, that I clearly did not have sufficient boldness or political experience at the time."

One muscovite recollected Yeltsin's answer five years later, commenting, "At the time I thought it was rather cheap. He was trying to win credit for having kept his mouth shut. But I now realize he was the only one who was even prepared to raise the issue of responsibility for the past."

In his 27th Party Congress speech Yeltsin broke one of the oldest taboos in Communist party protocol: he called for an end to privileges at all levels. This call for justice drew no support from his listeners and only further isolated Yeltsin politically. In retrospect, Morrison wrote, "The origin of the split between Gorbachev and Yeltsin can be seen in the populist tone of this speech and in Yeltsin's abrasive attitude to the party apparat [career bureaucrats], led by Ligachev."

During his two years as Moscow party chief, Yeltsin never ceased to be shocked and horrified by the corruption and nepotism that had infiltrated every establishment in

Moscow. For decades, Soviet propaganda in schools and in the press had promoted the idea that the standard of living in the Soviet Union surpassed that of any capitalist country. Nevertheless, Yeltsin saw how all the party elite fought fiercely to place their children in overseas jobs and to obtain permission to go on trips to Western Europe and the United States. These party members bought tape recorders, cameras, and other valuable items unavailable in the Soviet Union and sold them on the black market for a huge profit.

By Yeltsin's second year in office, the tension between him and the conservatives at Politburo meetings had mounted, and Yeltsin found himself more and more ostracized at the meetings. A major clash developed between Yeltsin and Ligachev, who had instituted an antialcoholism campaign (with Gorbachev's approval). Yeltsin felt that the whole campaign was, "simply amazingly ill conceived and ridiculous." Yeltsin concluded that no one was really drinking less alcohol, and that the money from the sale of liquor was not going to the state but rather to the black market and the moonshiners themselves. Yeltsin also noted that the number of cases of alcoholic poisonings had risen dramatically, and many were fatal. Despite the fact that Yeltsin said conditions were serious, Ligachev continued to release optimistic reports on the success of the campaign.

Yeltsin thought Gorbachev must be aware of the false nature of Ligachev's reports, and he expected Gorbachev to stop the campaign. But Yeltsin did not sense how isolated he had become; Gorbachev no longer supported Yeltsin and considered his criticisms of the system and the reforms too destructive and negative. Gorbachev stormed out of a Politburo meeting in October 1987, just before the 70th anniversary of the Russian Revolution was to be celebrated on November 7, after Yeltsin criticized his speech. Half an hour later, Gorbachev returned to the meeting and began to verbally attack Yeltsin, accusing him

THE RIVALS: GORBACHEV AND YELTSIN

At the 27th Party Congress of February 1986, delegates from throughout the country clap along with General Secretary Gorbachev (center), who is flanked by Yegor Ligachev (left), secretary of the Central Committee, and Andrei Gromyko (right), president of the Soviet Union. At the Congress, Yeltsin (second row, left) delivered a speech criticizing the CPSU's elite for accepting party privileges.

of failing in his job in Moscow. About this confrontation Yeltsin wrote, "There can be no doubt that at that moment Gorbachev simply hated me. . . . But that was only the beginning. The beginning of the end . . . I was too obviously a misfit in his otherwise obedient team."

By the time Gorbachev turned on Yeltsin, the head of the city committee had few supporters left. One cardinal rule of Soviet politics had always been to be a team player, and Yeltsin had disregarded decades of tradition and policy. He felt a moral obligation to speak out, just as he had done in the past under very different circumstances when the stakes had been much lower. Yet the system would not put up with such an irritating dissident, and plans for his ouster began to be set in motion.

Even though most of the party elite quickly sided with Gorbachev and Ligachev in the conflict with Yeltsin, a few loyal supporters remained on the side of Yeltsin, even at the risk of losing their own jobs. Furthermore, Ligachev felt that Yeltsin owed him his loyalty because he had helped bring Yeltsin to Moscow. When Yeltsin had first purged the Moscow party apparat in 1985, he appointed Mikhail Poltaranin to be the editor of the newspaper *Moskovskaya Pravda*, and Poltaranin had remained an ardent supporter ever since. Poltaranin believed that Yeltsin's clash with the other Politburo members was inevitable. In 1991, looking back on these events, Poltaranin said:

> He was the same Yeltsin as today, with the same natural intuition and ability to keep his feet firmly on the ground.
>
> It was as if, when they became members of the Politburo, they passed through some kind of radioactive zone where everything human was squeezed out of them, and their personality got left behind at the gates of the Kremlin. Yeltsin should have been the same but the rays in the zone failed to demagnetize him. He came here from Sverdlovsk, where he had imagined people in Moscow were handling high affairs of state, and he discovered this shaika [criminal gang]—that's what they were in the Politburo, and he was really shocked by where he had ended up.

Yeltsin had been reluctant to come to Moscow initially, and now that he saw the mafialike nature of the government and the city, he refused to play into his enemies' hands or give into the threats and bribes that surrounded him. While Yeltsin's adversaries planned his ouster, Poltaranin received an order to go before the Central Committee, whose members demanded that he sign a false statement criticizing Yeltsin. In the statement, Poltaranin was to claim that Yeltsin had coerced him into printing critical articles. Poltaranin later said, "I refused. I spoke about this to Yeltsin himself. He replied: 'I know that they are digging my grave.'"

The rift between Gorbachev and Yeltsin went deeper than the superficial disagreements over policy issues, such as the alcoholism campaign. Their differences became apparent early on, in their upbringings, their attitudes towards the party, and Yeltsin's waning confidence in the Communist ideal. Until the very end of the dissolution of the Soviet Union, Gorbachev remained a true believer in communism, and he strove to keep the union together and to maintain Soviet, Communist rule. Yeltsin, on the other hand, changed during the 1980s, believing more and more in true democracy, ownership of private property, and a competitive market economy. Yeltsin criticized Gorbachev's attempt to "ride two horses at once" by trying to hold on to socialism while introducing partial capitalism and democracy. Yeltsin wanted Gorbachev to make the leap to the other side and renounce everything that was the essence of Communist rule, but Gorbachev could never let go of his basic belief in communism.

In 1987, Yeltsin realized his departure from the top had become inevitable, and he decided to resign from the Politburo. While Gorbachev was on vacation at his Black Sea dacha, Yeltsin wrote him a letter in which he offered his resignation. In the letter, Yeltsin pleaded with Gorbachev to do something about Ligachev and the snail's pace that perestroika was taking. He also criticized himself—his style, his blunt, frank manner, and his inflexibility on issues of principle. He wrote, "I am an awkward person and I know it. I realise, too, that it is difficult for you to decide what to do about me." Yeltsin had always felt like an outsider, and now he admitted to Gorbachev that he just could not fit in any longer. Ultimately, Yeltsin hoped that Gorbachev would see his letter as a call to action, and that instead of accepting his resignation Gorbachev would ally himself with Yeltsin's reformist forces. Yeltsin realized, however, that he was taking a big risk, and he might not convince Gorbachev to come over to his side.

Maverick politician Yeltsin addresses a session of the Russian Congress. Yeltsin had attempted to resign from his position in Moscow at the October 1987 meeting of the Central Committee in which he gave a speech denouncing the failure of Gorbachev's reform programs.

6

The Yeltsin Affair

WHEN GORBACHEV RECEIVED Yeltsin's letter of resignation during his vacation, he probably considered the whole question of Yeltsin's leaving a nuisance and wanted to postpone dealing with it until after the November 7 celebration of the 70th anniversary of the Russian Revolution. Gorbachev's concern at the time was to present a picture of a cohesive and united Politburo. Gorbachev wanted the commemoration to show the world how well the Soviet government functioned. The last thing he wanted was a scandal about the firing or resignation of a high-ranking Politburo member with a high profile. Besides the consideration of the bad timing of Yeltsin's resignation, Gorbachev also wanted Yeltsin to help maintain the balance of radicals and conservatives in the Politburo in policy struggles over perestroika and glasnost. If Yeltsin left, the conservatives would dominate the Politburo and pressure Gorbachev to follow their advice.

Upon returning from his vacation, Gorbachev postponed his meeting with Yeltsin and left the question over his resignation open, telling him ambiguously on the phone, "Let's meet later." Yeltsin, however, decided to take matters into his own hands. At the next Central Committee meeting, in which the commemoration of the anniversary of the Russian Revolution was planned, he gave a speech and announced his resignation. Until Yeltsin addressed the Central Committee, the meeting had been composed of a well-organized series of self-congratulatory speeches and upbeat statements avoiding discussion of the current problems in Soviet society. Yeltsin's spontaneous speech came at the very end of the meeting and brought the celebratory nature of the gathering to a speedy halt. After Yeltsin's speech, the whole Politburo turned on him—even his closest allies—in an attempt to save themselves from being ostracized or criticized by Gorbachev.

Yeltsin wrote of the aftermath a few years later, "Even now, when so much time has passed, a rusty nail is still lodged in my heart and I have not pulled it out. It protrudes and it bleeds. I still find this hard to explain. Did I really expect anything else from the then largely conservative membership of the Central Committee? Of course I didn't; I knew the impending scenario only too well." Yeltsin realized he had no allies left: "Gorbachev would, so to speak, set the tone, then one accuser after another would come dashing up to the rostrum and would indict me for threatening party unity, for overweening ambition and for political intrigue."

Despite the attack, the committee still would not accept Yeltsin's resignation. They wanted to drag the process out, make Yeltsin pay for his "politically erroneous" speech. Yeltsin's speech marked the first open criticism of Gorbachev and his policies of perestroika and glasnost. In his autobiography, Yeltsin wrote, "At that time [October 1987], my speech was the first piece of criticism aimed at Gorbachev, the first attempt—not over the kitchen table but in a party forum—to discuss openly why perestroika was making no progress." Yeltsin's public criticism of Gorbachev, the hail of reproaches he received after his speech, the scandal of his attempted resignation, and his eventual ouster from the Politburo all came to be known as "The Yeltsin Affair." Yeltsin's actions broke every rule of Soviet protocol. Not only did he criticize the supreme Soviet leader but he asked to resign from the halls of power and privilege, an action unheard of in Soviet culture. In 1991, one Western observer wrote of this unprecedented event, "The subversive nature of his intervention lay not in his language, but in the way he broke the rules of the inner-Party game.... By resigning, he was saying goodbye to the dacha with its marble floors, the cooks, the gardeners, and the big black limousine—breaking the golden chains which were supposed to keep him in line."

About Yeltsin's bold move, former Soviet commentators Solovyov and Klepikova remarked:

> He was the only Soviet ruler who had ever made it to the top of the mountain, then hurried down back to the valley—of his own free will. That was his main breach of age-old Kremlin tradition: one could make the descent only by dying or being expelled. Great power automatically called for great slavery, and no Kremlin slave could simply shake off the chains of privilege. Yeltsin was the only person who ever considered it possible.

Yeltsin's speech and his attempt to extricate himself from the corruption and bootlicking he witnessed daily marked an important turning point not only for his career but for the beginning of the end of the Soviet Union as well.

On November 9, three weeks after his speech, Yeltsin collapsed from a heart attack. The Kremlin doctors pumped Yeltsin full of sedatives and other medication and forbade his wife from seeing him, claiming he was too ill to have any visitors. Two days later, while Yeltsin lay in bed in his hospital room, attached to an IV and full of tranquilizers, he received a telephone call from Gorbachev

Yeltsin waves to reporters as he walks in Moscow with his wife, Naya. Three weeks after his resignation speech to the Central Committee, Yeltsin suffered a heart attack. Kremlin doctors forbade Naya to visit her husband while he was in the hospital, insisting that he was too ill for any visitors.

(each of these "elite" hospital rooms had a special telephone link to the Kremlin). Yeltsin later recalled the phone call:

> It was Gorbachev, and he spoke as if he were not calling me in hospital but at my dacha. In a calm voice he asked me to go round and see him for a short while and then, perhaps, to attend the plenum of the Moscow city committee together. I said I couldn't come because I was in bed and the doctors wouldn't even let me get up. He told me cheerfully, telling me not to worry, that the doctors would help me to do so.... However much Gorbachev may have disliked me, to act like that was inhuman and immoral. I simply hadn't expected it of him.... Perhaps he actually wanted to finish me off physically? I could not understand such cruelty.

The doctors, who had ordered Yeltsin to stay in bed and had denied him visitors under orders from Gorbachev, gave Yeltsin even more sedatives, and despite his dizziness from fatigue and drugs, dragged him to a car and drove him to the Central Committee. According to Yeltsin, his wife, who witnessed this cruel treatment of her husband by Kremlin doctors and KGB agents, yelled at them, calling them sadists and cowards, but to no avail.

The meeting of the Central Committee, where Yeltsin tried to stand up and speak but could not articulate a full sentence, resembled a Stalinist show trial, with one important difference: Yeltsin would not be executed or sent to a labor camp afterwards. Times had changed dramatically, and he had become too well known by the general public and the press to actually be eliminated by forced retirement, or worse. Yeltsin's dismissal was painful and cruel, however, and the process took its toll. Yeltsin later described his ordeal:

> What do you call it, when a person is murdered with words? Because what followed was like a real murder. After all, I could have been dismissed in a sentence or two, then and there, at the plenum. But no; they had to enjoy the whole process of public betrayal.... If I hadn't been so heavily doped, of course, I would have fought back, I would have refuted the lies and shown up the treachery—yes, the treachery!—of everyone who spoke.... So I was dismissed, ostensibly at my own request, but it was done with such a ranting, roaring and screaming that it has left a nasty taste in my mouth to this day.

After the vicious attack, Yeltsin returned to the hospital. During his recovery there, Gorbachev tried to urge him to retire, but Yeltsin could not imagine giving up, and he fought off these suggestions. He would not consider retirement because he knew he would become bored, and he needed to be working with people. A little later, while Yeltsin still lay in the hospital, Gorbachev offered him the post of minister of Gosstroi, the state committee of construction, and Yeltsin immediately accepted it.

One question that still puzzles many observers of Russian politics today is why Gorbachev kept Yeltsin on in the

Moscow government when he had the power to force Yeltsin to retire or take a job far away from the center of Soviet politics. Yeltsin theorized that Gorbachev still wanted Yeltsin around to balance out the conservative and radical forces that vied for Gorbachev's approval. Yeltsin speculated that Gorbachev wanted him to remain in Moscow to keep "an inveterate opponent close by." Gorbachev needed someone like Yeltsin to foil the old hard-liners. Yeltsin commented on how he thought Gorbachev viewed the situation: "There is the conservative Ligachev, who plays the villian; there is Yeltsin, the bully-boy, the madcap radical; and the wise, omniscient hero is Gorbachev himself."

Even though Yeltsin had a job, he had been completely removed from the political arena, and all his former colleagues shunned him. Yeltsin fell into a deep mental depression following his recovery from the heart attack. When he voiced his criticisms in the Politburo, he knew he would meet with some resistance and conservative opposition, but he had no idea that being honest would lead to complete isolation and rejection. He wrote in *Against the Grain* that it felt as though he had some contagious disease or that he did not exist.

Yeltsin could not sleep. He had terrible headaches and often fell into bad moods. During these difficult months, his family consoled him and tried to help him through his depression. Burned-out and disillusioned, Yeltsin had few doctors he could trust anymore, and his mental depression only exacerbated his physical weakness. A few loyal friends still visited him during this period, and he admitted that he "was not quite on a desert island."

Gradually, Yeltsin started putting his life back together. He began going for walks around the city, unencumbered by bodyguards or political aides. Everywhere he went, ordinary people recognized him and treated him cordially—a sharp contrast to his former colleagues. Even though Yeltsin went to work every day and took solace in his walks around Moscow, he called this period, which lasted for 18 months, a nightmare. Not one to accept defeat, Yeltsin slowly began to piece together a strategy for his political comeback. Never before in the history of the Soviet Union, or prerevolutionary Russia for that matter, had anyone, after being defeated in a political battle, succeeded in reemerging into the world of politics and in rising to even greater heights of power than he had previously held.

During his political exile, Yeltsin received many requests from Western reporters for interviews. Soviet reporters tried to write about him, too, but the censors prevented any interviews or news about him from being published in the Soviet Union. Yeltsin gave a few interviews to the Western press, but these exchanges only led to reprimands from the party for making statements that might damage the image of the Soviet Union.

On one occasion, Yeltsin met with a group of young students at the Higher Komsomol School for a general discussion of economic issues. The meeting lasted for five hours and it confirmed how eager the Soviet people really were to discuss the same subjects that Yeltsin had dared to broach at Politburo meetings. Later, Yeltsin wrote, "I knew in advance that the occasion would be fraught with risk, and this turned out to be the case. I began by making a speech, taking a general look at various political, economic and social problems, and describing the processes that were taking place within the party . . . I even answered questions about Gorbachev's failings, which at the time was almost unthinkable."

Despite many changes in Soviet society, the KGB still functioned much as it always had—Yeltsin's entire meeting with the Komsomol students was taped. The only time Yeltsin met Gorbachev during his political exile—and it was an accidental meeting—Gorbachev asked him about the Komsomol gathering. Gorbachev was unquestionably keeping tabs on this troublemaker.

The Komsomol meeting, and his subsequent brief exchange with Gorbachev indicated to Yeltsin that he still had a good chance of reemerging in the political arena. Yeltsin later wrote, "I had the feeling that the ice was breaking up. My incarceration was coming to an end. New times were on the way, unpredictable and unfamiliar, in which I had to find a place for myself."

During Yeltsin's 18 months in political exile, the Soviet economy continued to plummet. Losses in productivity, rises in prices, and the collapse of the supply system all appeared imminent. Western observers thought that Gorbachev seemed to have lost sight of his strategy, and that he no longer controlled the workings of the system. Meanwhile, the Soviet people became more disillusioned than ever.

Yeltsin had an opportunity for a possible comeback in 1988, when the 19th Party Conference planned to convene. (Party Congresses, which met every five years, were planned general meetings, mandated by the CPSU rules. Party Conferences, on the other hand, met only under extraordinary circumstances, when an important issue needed to be resolved before the next scheduled congress. Party Conferences always focused on a particular issue; the special theme of the 19th Party Conference centered on Gorbachev's reforms.) Yeltsin wanted to be elected as a delegate to this conference, but the party apparat worked hard to prevent his election. Yeltsin succeeded at the last minute in becoming a delegate for the tiny autonomous republic of Karelia (within the larger republic of Russia). Other radicals and supporters of Gorbachev's reforms also had difficulty securing positions as delegates—the conservatives in the party tried vehemently to monopolize the conference. But times had changed. Democracy had started to infiltrate the age-old totalitarian walls of the Kremlin. John Morrison described the importance of this conference in *Boris Yeltsin: From Bolshevik to Democrat*:

THE YELTSIN AFFAIR

The Nineteenth Party Conference was the first gathering since the 1920s to break the pattern of well-scripted unanimity at the top of Soviet politics. For the first time, there would be spontaneity and disagreements; not everything would be pre-ordained from above. And the political balance had shifted from the moment, eight months earlier, when Yeltsin had been shot down in flames. Unlike a closed-door Central Committee meeting, the conference was a public and televised occasion.

When Yeltsin heard Gorbachev address the conference, he probably felt a certain satisfaction at hearing his former

An elderly woman tries to exchange her sweater for a fish at a flea market in Moscow. During Yeltsin's 18 months in political exile, he saw the Soviet economy plummet, with losses in productivity and rises in prices, and the looming collapse of the supply system.

patron repeat some of his own ideas. Calling for a cardinal reform of the Soviet political system, Gorbachev acknowledged that perestroika had essentially failed to get society moving. Although he could not obtain official permission to address the conference, Yeltsin successfully made his way to the rostrum and demanded to be given a chance to speak his mind. In his speech, Yeltsin first cleared up a few misinforming rumors about the so-called Yeltsin Affair and repeated his demand for Ligachev's resignation. He then went on to give a clear, well thought-out speech about some of the problems facing the Soviet Union. He called for elections by secret ballot for the presidencies of each republic, and for each presidency to last a maximum of two terms and to require an age limit of 65. Although he did not suggest instituting a multiparty system in this speech, Yeltsin would later advocate this essential aspect of democracy. He also raised the issue of the general secretary's immunity from criticism, a taboo subject, during his speech. Yeltsin himself was the very example of what happens to someone who dares to criticize Gorbachev. Next, he discussed the stratified nature of the Soviet economy and the prevailing low standard of living of the majority of the population. "In my opinion," Yeltsin said, "the principle should be as follows: if there is a lack of anything in our socialist society, then that shortage should be felt in equal degree by everyone without exception." Yeltsin also suggested that the party apparat be trimmed and redundant jobs eliminated. Finally, he asked the delegates to grant him political rehabilitation.

When Yeltsin finished his speech, he received warm support from many of his fellow delegates. Gorbachev and Ligachev organized another retaliatory attack on Yeltsin after his speech, but this time the tides had turned. The whole conference was being televised, and public opinion supported Yeltsin and his recommendations.

Ligachev gave a speech after Yeltsin and tried to put Yeltsin down, but he only succeeded in putting his foot in his mouth when he inadvertently criticized Gorbachev by saying he agreed with Yuri Bondarev, a conservative writer, who had compared perestroika to a plane that takes off without the pilot knowing where he is going. Reflecting on Ligachev's speech, Morrison wrote, "The speech was a self-inflicted defeat. Ligachev abandoned normal rules of politeness by addressing Yeltsin not as 'Boris Nikolayevich' but as plain 'Boris,' like a teacher speaking to a schoolboy. . . . The virulence of his attack came over badly on television."

While Ligachev set in motion his own defeat, Yeltsin took further steps towards his recovery. Yeltsin's bold, brazen character helped him maintain hope during his darkest hours and enabled him to summon the courage to demand a hearing, even though he had been repeatedly shunned and silenced by others.

Nevertheless, the 19th Party Conference did not grant Yeltsin political rehabilitation, and the conservative forces within the party had no intention of forgiving him. The Soviet people, however, had already begun to respect and support Yeltsin. The televised battle with the apparat helped people see that Yeltsin understood their frustration with the inequalities of Soviet society. Yeltsin became a hero—he was the first man to take on the monopoly of the Communist party and survive.

In 1990, Russian Orthodox Christians carry a photograph of Czar Nicholas II as they parade past a giant poster of Lenin in Mosow. They assembled for the blessing of the cornerstone of a cathedral that was destroyed by the Communists in 1936 and is to be rebuilt.

7

From Communist to Democrat

THE OCTOBER 1987 SPEECH that triggered the Yeltsin Affair had been far more prescient than Yeltsin could have imagined. Almost a year later, in September 1988, Gorbachev purged the Politburo of many conservative opponents, including Ligachev, forcing them to retire. Because Gorbachev's actions followed Yeltsin's recommendations, they helped vindicate Yeltsin.

The Soviet economy continued to worsen, and a serious earthquake that shook northwestern Armenia on December 7, 1988, only aggravated Gorbachev's problems. The government did not adequately or efficiently respond to the earthquake victims—55,000 of whom died—and Soviet doctors were unable to cope with the high number of casualties, thus exposing the abysmal quality of Soviet health care. International communities and organizations responded swiftly and sympathetically, but the catastrophe only added to Gorbachev's tainted reputation at home.

After Gorbachev reorganized the Politburo, he called for the creation of a new advisory body, the Congress of People's Deputies, which would function as a union parliament, separate from the Communist party. This Congress would have a multicandidate, secret ballot election in March 1989. Gorbachev and the top party *apparatchiks*, however, insisted on maintaining a provision from the previous party system that would prevent them from being subject to a public vote. Two-thirds of the seats would be filled by popular vote, and the remaining third would be occupied by the party—thus preventing Gorbachev and the other party officials from facing public scrutiny or rejection. Gorbachev's establishment of this new Congress represented an attempt to break the monopoly of power that the party had over all aspects of Soviet life. He wanted to initiate partial democracy into Soviet politics, but not at the risk of being voted out of office himself. Even these small concessions towards democracy, however, had repercussions far beyond Gorbachev's intentions. Morrison commented on the power of the popular vote, writing in his book on Yeltsin that Gorbachev had reduced the effectiveness of the party in all aspects of Soviet life out of preference for a new organization that he would find even harder to manage. Gorbachev's mastery in maneuvering set in motion processes that would eventually pare down his power. "Democracy," Morrison wrote, "was a game where someone else might turn out the winner."

Just as when Yeltsin had fought the party apparat for a seat at the 19th Party Conference, the conservative opposition put up a nasty battle to keep Yeltsin out of the new parliament. This time, however, Yeltsin sensed how much support he had and persisted in his effort to become a representative of Moscow (instead of a tiny city or region). Yeltsin waged a strong election campaign in Moscow, and despite the party's efforts to thwart him, he won 89 percent of the vote. Of the 6.8 million people who voted, 5.1 million voted for Yeltsin, while only 400,000 voted for the other candidate. The March 1989 vote marked the first democratic election in Russia since 1917, and Yeltsin's victory indicated how overwhelming the people's hate was for the old-style party system and how they longed to do away with it.

The Russian people supported Yeltsin for a number of reasons. First, Yeltsin's honesty appealed to them. The Russian people had been lied to for so long that Yeltsin's straightforward nature came as a pleasant shock to many. Second, Yeltsin had renounced party privileges and had shown real concern for the common people. Also, he did not pretend to have all the answers, and he asked people for their support and their ideas instead of lecturing and intimidating them. Finally, Yeltsin had courageously resigned from a high office and had displayed bravado before the party—this boldness gave him a huge following.

The Congress of People's Deputies opened on May 25, 1989, and lasted for three weeks. Although the Congress did function as the embryonic beginning of a democracy in the Soviet Union, for the time being Gorbachev still held the reins of power. When Gorbachev disapproved of a speech, such as the one the dissident scientist Andrei Sakharov had given on the last day of the gathering when he criticized the inability of the Congress to make real changes, Gorbachev ordered Sakharov's microphone to be disconnected, shouting, "That's enough!"

Despite Gorbachev's dominance, Yeltsin succeeded in being elected to the Supreme Soviet (the executive leadership) of the Parliament. Yeltsin's election and his growing popularity posed a threat to Gorbachev, who still had never been put to the test of a public vote and who increasingly seemed out of touch with the needs of the people. For Yeltsin, election to the Congress signaled his own resurrection in politics. Yeltsin wrote in his autobiography:

> I sometimes feel that I have lived three different lives: the first, although not without its difficulties and tensions, was nevertheless much like other people's lives—study; work;

Yeltsin gestures beside dissident scientist Andrei Sakharov during the November 28, 1989, session of the Supreme Soviet. Six months earlier, at a CPSU Congress session, President Gorbachev had disapproved of Sakharov's pro-democracy speech and had his microphone disconnected before Sakharov could complete his address.

family; a career as an industrial manager, then as a party official. It ended on the day of the October 1987 plenum of the Central Committee. Then began my second life—as a political outcast, surrounded by a void, a vacuum. I found myself cut off from people and had to struggle to survive, both as a human being and as a politician. Then, on the day that I won the election as a people's deputy, my third life began—it was my third birth, as it were.

In September 1989, a few months after the Congress of People's Deputies met, Yeltsin took his first trip to the United States. The trip lasted only nine days, from September 9–18, but it made a lasting impression on Yeltsin. He had traveled a few times before to Czechoslovakia, West Germany (now Germany), Cuba, and Nicaragua, but he remained relatively inexperienced in the world of diplomatic traveling, and he tried to prepare for the trip to the United States by meeting with Soviet academics who specialized in American politics. Despite his preparations, Yeltsin overbooked himself, visiting 11 cities in one week and lecturing and giving news conferences at most of his stops. At first, Yeltsin enjoyed the trip and found the United States an exciting, impressive country. After sightseeing in New York City he told a journalist from the *Washington Post*, "It appears that capitalism is not rotting away, as we were told, but it seems to be prospering. The Statue of Liberty is not some sort of a witch, but a very attractive lady."

What impressed Yeltsin the most during his trip to the United States was something that most Americans take for granted: a grocery store. Yeltsin wrote that he was shocked by the abundance of food, "When I saw those shelves crammed with hundreds, thousands of cans, cartons and goods of every possible sort, for the first time I felt quite frankly sick with despair for the Soviet people. That such a potentially super-rich country as ours has been brought to a state of such poverty. It is terrible to think of it." Yeltsin also found, to his surprise, that most Americans he met were optimistic and patriotic, characteristics he had not expected.

As the trip wore on, Yeltsin started to show signs of fatigue from the grueling schedule and from jet lag. After a brief, unofficial meeting with President George Bush's national security adviser, Brent Scowcroft, and an informal visit by the president himself, the American press started to criticize Yeltsin. A *New York Times* reporter wrote that Yeltsin's proposals to the U.S. leadership, "went down like a lead pirogi." But that statement marked only the beginning of a smear campaign that reached its height with Paul Hendrickson's article in the *Washington Post* entitled, "Boris's Boozy Bear Hug for the Capitalists." Hendrickson wrote that Yeltsin was actually a cloddy alcoholic trying to make his way through the corridors of American power. He then went on to criticize Yeltsin's appearance, "he has an elastic face that would have been perfect on a '40s burlesque stage. His silver hair has a wondrous upsweep. His nose is a proboscis. He wears his watch on the inside of his wrist. The voice volume is enough to shatter dishes."

Upon his return to Moscow, Yeltsin found out that a similar article, which appeared in the newspaper *Pravda*

On September 17, 1989, Yeltsin shows his astonishment at the selection in the frozen food section of a Houston, Texas, grocery store during his first visit to the United States. He was shocked by the abundance of food in U.S. stores and later said, "I felt quite frankly sick with despair for the Soviet people."

(and had been translated from an article in an Italian newspaper), had lambasted his behavior on the trip, claiming he had been drunk the whole time, and that he spent all his lecture fees on luxuries in the United States. In fact, Yeltsin had donated all his lecture fees to the Soviet anti-AIDS campaign to buy a million syringes.

Yeltsin had expected a negative reaction from his opponents, but he was shocked by the viciousness of these attacks. He wrote of this article, "[It] made me look like the usual drunken, lumbering, ill-mannered Russian bear at his first encounter with civilized society." Nevertheless, Yeltsin's popularity remained steadfast. He received thousands of letters and telegrams of support, and a written apology from *Pravda*. The Italian journalist also apologized and admitted that his piece had mainly been a rewrite of Hendrickson's *Washington Post* article.

Yeltsin's trip to the United States forced him to realize that in the game of politics one had to be on guard at all times. A month later, in October, an incident occurred that appeared to be yet another attempt to tarnish Yeltsin's reputation. Yeltsin's account of the controversial episode went as follows: he had gone out to the country to visit a friend, and while walking alone along a river bank, a car suddenly appeared and chased him into the icy river. After dragging himself out of the water, Yeltsin stumbled to a nearby police station. He decided not to make an official statement because he was worried that a report of an attempt on his life might result in a huge public protest by his supporters.

Initially, it seemed that the public resented Yeltsin's decision not to come forward and explain what had happened, believing that his silence added to the suspicion that he might be an alcoholic. Morrison, however, noted a few years later that the incident actually endeared Yeltsin to the Russian people even more: "For many Russians, it confirmed his larger-than-life image as a man who might occasionally have one glass too many and get into a scrape.

Yeltsin's popularity was too strong to be permanently damaged by stories about him losing his balance or his trousers. Yeltsin treated the incident as part of the price of remaining in politics."

While Yeltsin strove to make up for lost time by traveling in 1989 both within the Soviet Union and to the United States, Eastern Europe changed rapidly from a block of Soviet-dominated Socialist countries to a disparate group of independent countries with their governments in flux. The year 1989 marked the overthrow of Communist rule by the people in most of the countries of Eastern Europe—with relatively little bloodshed. Gorbachev, even though he believed strongly in socialism and in preventing the Soviet Union from breaking apart, did not try to intervene in any of the revolutions occurring in Eastern Europe. Each country emerged as a democratic nation in a different way—some through elections, others through mass demonstrations—but the results were the same. Poland, Czechoslovakia, Hungary, Yugoslavia, Bulgaria, and East Germany all renounced communism. Gorbachev also agreed to withdraw Soviet troops from these countries. The Baltic republics of Lithuania, Latvia, Estonia, and the republic of Moldavia all began to try to shake off Soviet rule, following the actions of neighboring Eastern Europe.

The representatives at the Congress of People's Deputies decided that a year later, in March 1990, they would hold elections in every republic to choose the heads of parliament for each republic. Technically, these elections were for the Chairmen of the Supreme Soviets of each republican parliament, but actually these elected officials acted as the main representatives of each republic in all-union negotiations with the central government. When Yeltsin ran for the position of Chairman of the Russian Supreme Soviet and won, he became, in effect, the first elected leader of Russia. However, direct presidential elections for each republic had not occurred yet. The Russian

On May 1, 1990, thousands of Muscovites march through Red Square, chanting support for Lithuania, which denounced seven decades of Communist rule. Lithuania was the first of the Baltic republics to establish a multiparty system of government.

republic held its election for the Supreme Soviet on March 4. This time Gorbachev and the party could not reserve a third of the seats, and the election process was far more democratic.

In the three Baltic republics, the election results indicated that there was strong discontent among the people. The local Communists were pushed out by popular fronts (groups of native Balts who wanted independence). A multiparty system had emerged. Nevertheless, the Communist party still existed, and the power structure of the country had hardly changed. At the next meeting of the Communist party, at the 28th Party Congress on July 12, 1990, Yeltsin delivered a farewell speech to the party in which he warned, "the question facing this Congress is primarily that of the fate of the CPSU itself. To be more precise, the only question being tackled here is the fate of the apparatus of the party upper echelons."

At the end of the Congress, Yeltsin resigned from the Communist party. Deciding to leave the party had not been easy for him. Earlier he had admitted to a *Pravda* reporter, "But on the other hand I have been in the Party for thirty years. And it is very, very difficult to make this decision. All this time I have had a great doubt when making this decision. I have constantly put it off." After the Congress, Yeltsin told another reporter in Latvia, "I could not stop thinking. I had colossal doubts, but I could do nothing else. After all, I have always said that a one-party monopoly is harmful to society, that it should be placed under the control of the legislative powers."

Morrison later explained Yeltsin's struggle with his decision to resign from the party: "There were, however, sound tactical reasons for Yeltsin to tone down his anti-Communist rhetoric and make his breach with the CPSU as smooth as possible. He did not want to antagonize the powerful Communist bloc in the Russian parliament, whose cooperation was essential to elect a functioning government." Yeltsin had joined the party as a young man, out of true conviction. But after 30 years in the party's fold, he did not regret his decision to leave. He said of his departure, "No, it was not a tragedy but rather a liberation from a false religion."

The transformation of the Soviet bloc (Eastern Europe) and the decline of the Communist party contributed to the public's concern about the USSR's fate. Could the union stay together? Or were the forces of change and democratization too strong? Gorbachev believed adamantly in maintaining the unity of the country, but many conservatives felt that his liberalization campaigns would lead inevitably to the breakup of the Soviet Union. Yeltsin foresaw the need for each republic to have sovereignty over its own affairs, even if the union still existed. Gradual-

On May 29, 1990, Yeltsin watches election results for the presidency of the Russian republic. Yeltsin won the election on the third ballot, making him the leader of the largest, most populous, and richest Soviet republic. His election helped to shift the balance of power away from Gorbachev, and several of the republics declared their sovereignty.

ly, Gorbachev found himself being caught up in a trap. The conservatives turned against him because they felt he was too much of a reformer, whereas the liberals believed he was not pushing for the reforms enough. The liberals called for a dissolution of power from the center, a move that Gorbachev felt would destroy the union. As Gorbachev tried to decide which route to take and how much power to give up to the individual republics, his time started to run out. The elections that took place in 1990, especially Yeltsin's (because he now headed the largest, most populous, and richest republic), shifted the balance of power away from Gorbachev. Although the republics of Russia, the Ukraine, and Byelorussia did not want to break up the union, they all declared their sovereignty and they demanded a new union treaty. By March 1990 Lithuania declared its independence. The Lithuanians did not want to sign a union treaty; they wanted to split off from the union completely.

Gorbachev's power continued to slip. His presidential orders went unnoticed and unfulfilled, and although he realized his authority was diminishing, he still could not decide which path to take. Gorbachev had always been a committed Communist, and he could not imagine letting go of his ideals. Moreover, even though he believed the breakup of the Soviet Union was inevitable, he felt that allowing it would lead to civil war.

The hard-liners in the Soviet army became more and more disillusioned and angry with Gorbachev's indecision. On January 13, 1991, 13 people were killed in Lithuania in a struggle between civilian separatists and the Soviet army. A week later, a similar incident in Latvia resulted in the deaths of five civilians. In both cases, Gorbachev claimed he had not ordered the killings, and his admission revealed how little control he actually had left. From the very beginning of the Baltic republics' struggle for independence, Yeltsin supported the republics' actions, even though he would have liked to have kept the union together in some kind of loose confederation. When violence erupted, Yeltsin became even more adamant in his support for Baltic independence.

During the Baltic crisis, Yeltsin told reporters, "We are worried that events could develop that could make it essential—as some people already think—for the army also to restore order. We regard this as an unprecedented thing, as an instance of forcible interference, as evidence of pressure on an independent, self-governing state." Yeltsin knew only too well that if the army could "restore order" in the Baltics by using violence, it could do so in Russia as well. "This is the next Afghanistan. We have already had Tbilisi [Georgia], Azerbaijan, Armenia, Fergana, and so on [places where the army had intervened]. To have yet another bloody wound on our already lacerated body is of course unacceptable."

With fist clenched, Yeltsin leads a group of antigovernment demonstrators in a march following a military parade in November 1990. Yeltsin realized that Gorbachev's desire to retain some of the old ideas of communism while introducing new reforms just would not work.

On June 19, 1991, Yeltsin wears a cowboy hat that was presented to him by U.S. Senate minority leader Robert Dole of Kansas during Yeltsin's second visit to Washington, D.C.

8

The Collapse of an Empire and the Birth of a Nation

IN RETROSPECT, THE FIRST HALF of 1991 included a number of political events that foreshadowed the coup attempt of August 19. Two main concerns threatened the conservative forces in the Kremlin and in the Soviet army and eventually led them to try to overthrow the government. The first concern involved the breakup of the Soviet Union and the republics' growing demand for more autonomy from Moscow. The second was the election of Yeltsin as president of Russia.

Tensions between the republics and Gorbachev continued to mount. In March 1991, 300,000 miners went on strike in the rich coal-mining regions of Northern Russia. The miners demanded Gorbachev's resignation, better working conditions, and higher pay. Gorbachev, in his negotiations with the miners, refused to step down, but he soon found that he needed Yeltsin's help in settling the crisis. Yeltsin suggested transferring all the mines to Russia's control, and he openly sympathized with the miners' grievances. Gorbachev had to agree to many of the miners' demands and to the transfer of control of the mines to Russia because the strikes soon spread to other republics and threatened to bring the ailing Soviet economy to a screeching halt.

Attempts to create a federation of loosely joined states intensified the stress between the republics and Gorbachev, who had now become a very unpopular figure because of his inability to relinquish power at the center. Yeltsin, on the other hand, grasped the new reality and openly campaigned for more autonomy for the republics. In March 1991, he gave a speech to the Russian Parliament in which he came close to advocating the dissolution of the Soviet Union. Full of his characteristic ardor, he told the Parliament, "the objective outcome of the past six years has shown that we were dealing not with perestroika, but with the last phase of stagnation." He went on to say that there had been some progress made, namely that the Soviet people had changed—they now understood the truth about their society and their history, and about how people in other countries lived. The Soviet people no

Striking miners in Vorkuta gather outside a mine shaft after the Soviet Parliament voted to suspend the miners' strike on March 26, 1991. More than 300,000 miners had demanded Gorbachev's resignation, improved working conditions, and better pay.

longer tolerated the old totalitarian system; they were beginning to convert to democratic ideas.

Yeltsin conceded, nonetheless, that the forces of democracy still had a long way to go because the CPSU still controlled the country. He had to admit that he did not advocate unseating Gorbachev, because the democrats had not yet become a full-scale political party. Morrison commented on the party's control during this period, writing, "the CPSU today remains the ruling party, with all its property and power, and the KGB and the army. Everything belongs to it."

In April 1991, the remaining nine republican representatives of Russia (also referred to as the Russian Federation), Kazakhstan, Azerbaijan, Kirghizia, Uzbekistan, Tadzhikistan, Turkmenistan, the Ukraine, and Byelorussia signed a statement, known as the nine-plus-one agreement, with Gorbachev. The "nine" referred to these nine republics and the "one" alluded to the Soviet government,

On March 25, 1991, Yeltsin shakes hands with local representatives of the Ingush people in southern Russia while meeting with refugees from a Georgian district that wished to break away from Georgian rule. In April, Russia and eight other republics signed the nine-plus-one agreement, vowing to work with Gorbachev to ease the growing political tensions in the USSR.

located in Moscow. In this communiqué, the nine republics vowed to work with the central government in Moscow to try to stabilize the situation in the Soviet Union. The statement also called upon miners and other workers not to strike or to incite civil disobedience. In addition, the agreement promised to develop a "treaty of sovereign states," which would entail a new constitution and new elections within each state. The six states that had declared their independence—Estonia, Latvia, Lithuania, Georgia, Armenia, and Moldavia—would be able to join the new treaty if they so desired.

All of the coup plotters had been excluded from the negotiations for the nine-plus-one agreement, and they staged the coup attempt on the eve of the signing of the treaty of sovereign states. Clearly, the plotters hoped to reinstate centralized power and nullify any agreements made for state sovereignty.

Earlier in the year, a nationwide referendum had approved the idea of a direct presidential election in each republic. Russia, being the largest, richest, and most influential of the remaining republics, posed the biggest threat to the center. When the Russian election finally took place in June 1991, Yeltsin won by a large margin. During the election, Gorbachev, who had made peace with Yeltsin, did not take sides, and this only added to the conservatives' anger towards him. Yeltsin, too, had stopped taking sides, now that the political tide was so clearly in his favor. On the campaign trail, reporters asked him whether he preferred socialism or capitalism, but he refused to champion either ideology. "When I am asked during my trips, 'Are you for socialism or capitalism?'" Yeltsin told a reporter, "I say: I am in favor of Russians living better—materially, spiritually, and culturally. A healthy society is determined by how people live, how they work, and how they are provided for materially, culturally, and intellectually. As for the name, people will think one up."

Gorbachev had lost much of his influence in domestic affairs, but he still held the reins in foreign policy. In mid-April, prior to the election, Yeltsin traveled to France, where he tried to meet with French officials. They had snubbed him and made it clear that they only recognized one president—Gorbachev. Richard Nixon—the former president of the United States who had become an outsider after the Watergate scandal in which he was forced to resign the presidency in 1974—was one of the few politicians willing to meet with Yeltsin before his election to the presidency. Nixon came away surprisingly impressed with Yeltsin, and said:

> After being led to expect a lightweight and a demagogue, I quickly realized how inaccurate media reports and assessments by establishment diplomats can be. The Russian

Inside the Kremlin, Yeltsin (second from left) stands with Vice President Ruslan Khasbulatov during Yeltsin's inauguration as the president of Russia on July 10, 1991. Yeltsin became the first popularly elected president in the history of the Soviet Union.

leader projects steely determination and strength of conviction. He has the physical magnetism that is so important for an effective politician. He is not as intellectual and sophisticated as Gorbachev, but he is still a political heavyweight. Gorbachev appeals to the head, Yeltsin to the heart; Gorbachev dazzles his listeners, Yeltsin moves them. If, as some critics claim, Yeltsin were seeking power for his own sake, he could be a very dangerous dictator. Fortunately, his critics are wrong.

After his election as president on June 12, 1991, Yeltsin visited the United States a second time, from June 19 to June 21, and received a friendlier welcome than he had been given in 1989. Even though American politicians had started to accept Yeltsin as a leader to be reckoned with, President Bush reiterated the United States's commitment to Gorbachev.

Morrison, describing Yeltsin's meeting in Washington, D.C., reported, "In the White House Rose Garden, President Bush praised Yeltsin's election victory but went on to deliver an extraordinary hymn of praise to Gorbachev, promising that the United States would maintain the 'closest possible official relationship' with his government. It was Gorbachev 'who enabled us to end the Cold War and make Europe whole and free,' said Bush." Yeltsin, not wishing to offend and realizing that he must not burn any bridges, said he would continue to support Gorbachev in his struggle against conservative forces. Yeltsin also told Bush, "Russia, which accounts for 70 percent of the gross national product of the Soviet Union, is strongly and irrevocably committed to democracy and it will not allow any reversal of history."

When Gorbachev returned from his dacha after the August 19 coup attempt, the Western world sighed in relief to see he had not been physically harmed by the plotters. In the Soviet Union, however, Gorbachev's return did not elicit such a warm reaction. The "Gorbymania" that had once excited Americans and Western Europeans had long since died in the USSR. Gorbachev's return only emphasized how helpless and out of touch with the people he had become before and during the coup attempt. He had lost credibility and legitimacy, and he soon realized the time had come for him to resign. Gorbachev left office in December 1991, and the Soviet Union ceased to exist.

The failure of the August coup sealed the fate of the Soviet Union and of Gorbachev. The union had been hanging on by a thread, but the disastrous coup attempt and Yeltsin's charismatic defense of democracy changed the course of history. Yeltsin clearly gained his powerful position through hard work, perseverance, and aggressiveness, but what made him unique in the history of the Soviet Union was his faith in the power of democracy.

Yeltsin put his own fate in the hands of the people. He ran on a platform that called for democratic elections and an end to party dominance. In addition, he lived by the values he espoused, gaining enormous credibility and popularity for his consistency. A Western observer of the Soviet Union explained the significance of Yeltsin's election by saying that "the vote further shifted the balance of legitimacy away from Gorbachev, who had never stood in a popular election, and toward Yeltsin, who had now done so three times." Yeltsin's triumph was not just a personal one—it was also a turning point in Russian history. Russians, for the first time ever, could wield popular sovereignty by selecting their own leader. The June 1991 election buried any remaining doubts about the people's renunciation of 74 years of communism, and of the "socialist choice" that Gorbachev still protected.

Yeltsin was "the first" on many levels. He succeeded in becoming the first democratically elected president of Russia. He also was the first person to dare to challenge the Soviet government from within. He became the first Politburo member to reject party privileges and perks. Yeltsin not only conceived of a political opposition to the one-party monopoly of the CPSU but also succeeded in breaking its stranglehold on the country. Two Russian reporters drew attention to Yeltsin's other "firsts," writing,

On August 23, 1991, Yeltsin points at Gorbachev while he addresses the Russian Parliament. Gorbachev lost all credibility and validity after the coup attempt, and in December he realized he had to resign from office.

"Yeltsin was the first Soviet leader to make a comeback from political limbo and to restart his career outside the ruling Party mechanism—through a direct appeal for grass-roots support." They also maintained that he was the only person among the ruling elite who had the revolutionary idea of Russia leaving the Soviet Union. Yeltsin was the first Soviet politician to take down Lenin's portrait from his office wall. Whenever someone came to visit him, Yeltsin would point at the empty spot on the wall and exclaim with a grin, "there's only a nail left." The reporters also explained that Yeltsin was "the first among several hundred Central Committee members to vote against the resolutions of Gorbachev's Politburo, thus destroying the illusion of unanimity in the party. It is an important part of his character: he is not afraid to go it alone, even if he is defying the entire world."

Yeltsin and his wife, Naya, have an audience with Pope John Paul II during a brief but historic visit to the Vatican on December 20, 1991.

Yeltsin is the leader of a country that is going through a very difficult transition. The Soviet state provided a level of security for every citizen that the new Russian state cannot guarantee. With the transition from a state-run economy to a privatized market economy, certain problems, such as unemployment and inflation, are inevitable. Moreover, the removal of many of the repressive elements of the totalitarian state has led to a precipitous rise in crime. Ethnic tensions have caused civil wars in some of the other former republics (such as Armenia, Azerbaijan, and Georgia) and have led to killing in the Russian territory as well. The Russian state is home to numerous ethnic and religious groups, and there have been a few violent incidents over territory within Russia's borders.

The new government is encouraging individual initiative, and the hope is that private investment and an entrepreneurial spirit will pull the economy out of the doldrums. Yeltsin likes to use South Korea and Japan as examples of countries that made a rapid transition from poor, underdeveloped nations to successful economies. While on the campaign trail, Yeltsin once said of these two countries:

> I am often faulted for taking South Korea and Japan as examples. Why not, if Koreans, who used oxen for transportation 40 years ago, are now living in one of the most developed countries in the world? . . . Japan is the richest country in the world. Can you imagine? GNP per capita is $24,000. In the United States, $18,000. In the Soviet Union, 6,000 . . . *rubles*. This is what we have to live on; this is what we have achieved. So what must be done? Denationalization of property, decentralization of everything—politics, economics, culture, everything.

Yeltsin has been received cordially by the United States and Western Europe, but he still has not elicited the same kind of passionate support that Gorbachev had overseas. The future of the loosely confederated Commonwealth of Independent States is also unclear. It remains to be seen how long the new arrangement of states can continue. The

Yeltsin jubilantly makes his way through a crowd after the failed coup on August 23, 1991. Yeltsin is unique in the history of the Soviet Union because he put his faith in the power of democracy and his fate in the hands of the people.

questions of how to dismantle the former Soviet Red Army and who will have control over nuclear weapons have been discussed peacefully by the leaders of the states, but new potential conflicts arise daily. At this writing, the Commonwealth of Independent States, and Russia in particular, appears less militaristic and far less expansionistic than the former Soviet Union. The focus of the new governments is on domestic problems and on how to rebuild the ailing economy. Struggles between the conservative forces of the former Soviet government and Yeltsin's more liberal, reform-minded supporters continue to threaten Yeltsin's authority as president of Russia. For example, in a session with the Congress of People's Deputies in December 1992, Yeltsin was forced to abandon his choice for prime minister, Yegor T. Gaidar, the chief architect of Yeltsin's radical economic program, because most members of Congress preferred a candidate who would take a more gradual path in transferring the country to a market economy.

Yeltsin continues to believe that the people of Russia will be the catalyst for recovery. On his trip to the United States in June 1991, Yeltsin spoke of this conviction to the National Press Club, saying, "I believe that Russia will be reborn. I believe that we shall see a rebirth of Russia, an economic rebirth, a spiritual rebirth of Russia, a human rebirth of Russia, that Russia will rediscover its ancient traditions which were once suppressed and trampled by the totalitarian empire built in our country since 1917."

The dismantling of the Soviet Union will take many years, and Yeltsin has few illusions about how difficult it will be. Despite all these challenges, Yeltsin has maintained his optimism and confidence as a leader. He has never been one to accept defeat, and he continues to believe in the power of democracy. Yeltsin still lives by a principle that he mentioned to a *London Times* reporter in 1990: "A man must live like a great bright flame and burn as brightly as he can. In the end he burns out. But this is better than a mean little flame."

Further Reading

Butson, Thomas. *Mikhail Gorbachev*. New York: Chelsea House, 1986.

Colton, Timothy, and Robert Legvold, eds. *After the Soviet Union*. New York: Norton, 1992.

Goldman, Marshall I. *What Went Wrong with Perestroika*. New York: Norton, 1991.

Gwertzman, Bernard, and Michael T. Kaufman, eds. *The Decline and Fall of the Soviet Empire*. New York: New York Times, 1992.

Lane, David. *Soviet Society Under Perestroika*. Revised edition. London: Routledge, 1992.

Morrison, John. *Boris Yeltsin: From Bolshevik to Democrat*. New York: Dutton, 1991.

Sheehy, Gail. *The Man Who Changed the World: The Lives of Mikhail S. Gorbachev*. New York: Harper Collins, 1990.

Smith, Hedrick. *The New Russians*. New York: Random House, 1990.

Solovyov, Vladimir, and Elena Klepikova. *Boris Yeltsin: A Political Biography*. New York: Putnam, 1992.

Yeltsin, Boris. *Against the Grain: An Autobiography*. London: Jonathan Cape, 1990.

Chronology

1917	Bolshevik socialism is established as the ruling power in the Soviet Union
1931	Born Boris Nikolayevich Yeltsin on February 1 in the village of Butko in Russia
1935	The Yeltsin family moves to Berezniki
1937	Nikolai Ignatievich, Yeltsin's father, is arrested by police, but is eventually released
1949	Yeltsin enters the Urals Polytechnic Institute in Sverdlovsk
1955	Graduates from the Urals Polytechnic Institute with a degree in civil engineering; begins training to become a construction foreman at a complex in Sverdlovsk
1956	Marries Anastasia (Naya) Girina
1957	Yeltsin's daughter, Lena, is born
1959	Daughter, Tanya, is born
1961	Yeltsin becomes head manager of construction complex; joins the Communist Party of the Soviet Union (CPSU)
1963	Becomes general manager of construction complex
1969	Becomes senior head of CPSU section, responsible for all construction in Sverdlovsk
1976	Meets Leonid Brezhnev and becomes first secretary of the Sverdlovsk CPSU; moves to Moscow
1985	Mikhail Gorbachev becomes general secretary of the CPSU and instigates his policies of *glasnost* and *perestroika*; Yeltsin becomes head of the Moscow city committee of the CPSU and a nonvoting member of the Politburo
1986	Yeltsin strongly criticizes CPSU corruption and the CPSU elite at a speech during the 27th Party Congress
1987	Gorbachev and Yeltsin clash at a Politburo meeting; "The Yeltsin Affair" commences when Yeltsin unsuccessfully attempts to resign from the Politburo during a speech to the Central Committee;

	Yeltsin suffers a heart attack three weeks later; he is expelled from the Politburo but is allowed to remain in Moscow as the minister of the state committee of construction; remains a political exile for the next 18 months
1988	Becomes a delegate to the 19th Party Conference; Gorbachev calls for the creation of a multiparty Congress of People's Deputies, with two-thirds of its membership to be democratically elected
1989	In March, despite CPSU opposition, Yeltsin is elected as Moscow's delegate to the Congress of People's Deputies with 89 percent of the vote; in May he is elected to the Supreme Soviet of the Congress; makes first visit to the United States
1990	On March 4, Yeltsin is elected Chairman of the Supreme Soviet of the Russian Parliament; on July 12, he resigns from the CPSU at the 28th Party Congress; various states begin to push for the dissolution of the Soviet Union in favor of independence or a looser confederacy
1991	Gorbachev appears to lose command of Soviet troops as they clash with Baltic separatists; Yeltsin becomes the first democratically elected President of Russia on June 12; hard-line Communists attempt a coup d'état on August 19 that Yeltsin's personal courage helps to defeat; Gorbachev resigns in December as the Soviet Union becomes the Commonwealth of Independent States
1992	Struggles between the conservatives of the former Soviet Union and Yeltsin's more liberal, reform-minded supporters threaten Yeltsin's authority as president when in December his choice for prime minister is rejected
1993	On March 10–13 the Congress of People's Deputies rejects a December compromise to hold an April 11 referendum to decide who will rule Russia; on March 20, Yeltsin declares special presidential rule and calls an April 25 constitutional referendum; on March 21, Parliament declares Yeltsin's actions unconstitutional but stops short of voting for impeachment; on April 25, a majority of the Russian people back Yeltsin in the national referendum

Index

Afghanistan, 51, 95
Against the Grain (Yeltsin), 27, 28, 32, 38, 41, 43, 44, 45, 49, 56, 65, 74, 78, 79
Andropov, Yuri, 52
Armenia, 56, 85, 95, 100
Azerbaijan, 95

Baklanov, Oleg, 16
Baltic republics, 91, 92, 95
Berezniki, Russia, 32, 34, 42
Bolshevik Revolution, 18, 29, 55, 68, 73, 74
Bolsheviks, 18, 24, 29
Bondarev, Yuri, 83
Boris Yeltsin: A Political Biography (Solovyov and Klepikova), 17
Boris Yeltsin: From Bolshevik to Democrat (Morrison), 54, 61, 80
Brezhnev, Leonid, 51, 52, 53, 54, 55
Bush, George, 19, 89, 102
Butko, Russia, 27

Censorship, 14, 50, 79
Central Committee, 67, 74, 77, 81, 104
Chernenko, Konstantin, 52
Cold war, 51, 57, 102
Collective farms, 29, 30, 32, 55
Collectivization, 29, 31, 33, 50
Commonwealth of Independent States, 25, 105, 106
Communism, 12, 13, 18, 24, 31, 43, 49, 51, 58, 62, 71, 95, 103
Communist Party Congress, 80
 19th, 80, 81, 83, 86

 20th, 50, 67
 22nd, 64
 26th, 67
 27th, 67
 28th, 92
Communist Party of the Soviet Union (CPSU), 24, 38, 40, 49, 53, 55, 56, 58, 61, 62, 63, 64, 65, 67, 75, 80, 83, 86, 91, 93, 99, 103, 104
Congress of People's Deputies, 86, 87, 88, 91, 93
Czechoslovakia, 51, 88, 91

Democracy, 14, 15, 19, 20, 24, 25, 71, 80, 86, 87, 99, 102, 103, 106
Détente, 51

Eastern Europe, 91, 93
Engels, Friedrich, 49
Europe, 58, 68, 102, 105

Gaidar, Yegor T., 106
Georgia, 56, 95, 100
Glasnost, 13, 14, 50, 52, 54, 66, 73, 74
Gorbachev, Mikhail, 12, 14, 15, 19, 20, 21, 23, 24, 52, 55, 73, 74, 76, 78, 79, 80, 81, 82, 83, 85, 91, 102, 104, 105
 early years, 61–63
 political career, 64, 94, 95, 98, 101, 103
 reorganizes Politburo, 86
 rivalry with Boris Yeltsin, 12, 25, 61–71, 87, 97, 99
Gosplan, 55
Great Britain, 11
Grishin, Viktor, 65

Hendrickson, Paul, 89

Kalinin, Mikhail, 58
Kazakhstan, 17
KGB (Komitet Gosudarstvennoi Bezopasnosti), 13, 15, 17, 19, 55, 77, 79
Khrushchev, Nikita, 49, 50, 51, 52, 64, 67
Klepikova, Elena, 17
Komsomol, 63, 64, 79, 80
Kravchenko, Leonid, 16
Kremlin, 16, 19, 20, 21, 23, 31, 50, 59, 70, 75, 76, 77, 80, 97
Kryuchkov, Vladimir, 16, 19

Latvia, 91, 93, 95, 100
Lenin, Vladimir Ilich, 18, 24, 29, 49, 50, 104
Leningrad, Russia, 18
Ligachev, Yegor, 65, 67, 68, 70, 71, 78, 82, 83, 85
Lithuania, 92, 94, 95, 100

Majors, John, 11
Marx, Karl, 49
Molotov, Vyacheslav, 58–59
Morrison, John, 54, 61, 64, 67, 80, 83, 86, 90, 93, 99, 102
Moscow, Russia, 14, 16, 18, 20, 22, 23, 24, 47, 53, 56, 62, 64, 65, 66, 67, 68, 69, 70, 78, 79, 86, 89, 97, 100
Moskovskaya Pravda, 70, 89, 93

New York City, 88
New York Times, 89
Nicaragua, 88
Nine-plus-one agreement, 99, 100
Nixon, Richard, 101

Orthodox Christianity, 29

Pavlov, Valentin, 16
Perestroika, 13, 14, 54, 66, 71, 73, 74, 75, 82, 83, 98
Politburo, 59, 65, 68, 70, 71, 73–79, 85, 103, 104
Pravda. See *Moskovskaya Pravda*
Presidential elections, 97, 100, 101, 103
Pugo, Boris, 16, 23

Russia, 11, 12, 13, 14, 23, 25, 61, 79, 80, 87, 99, 100, 102, 104, 105
Russian Federation, 99
Russian Parliament, 98, 106
Russian Revolution. See Bolshevik Revolution
Russian White House, 17, 18, 19

Sakharov, Andrei, 87
"Show trials," 34, 77
Solovyov, Vladimir, 17
Soviet bloc. See Eastern Europe
Soviet Red Army, 106
Soviet Union. See Union of Soviet Socialist Republics (USSR)
Stalin, Joseph, 20, 29, 31, 32, 33, 34, 50, 51, 58, 59, 64, 67
State Committee for the State of Emergency, 15
Stepankov, Valentin, 17
Supreme Soviet, 87, 91, 92
Sverdlovsk, Russia, 38, 42, 46, 53, 56, 64, 70

Times (London), 106

Tizyukov, Alexander, 16

Union of Soviet Socialist Republics (USSR), 11, 12, 13, 19, 20, 22, 29, 30, 31, 38, 41, 49, 50, 51, 52, 54, 55, 56, 58, 68, 79, 82, 86, 100, 102, 105, 106
   dissolution of, 15, 24, 25, 59, 71, 75, 93, 98, 104, 106
United States, 19, 20, 22, 51, 58, 63, 64, 68, 90, 91, 101, 102, 105, 106
Ural Mountains, 27, 29, 39
Urals Polytechnic Institute, 38, 41, 42, 43, 46

Washington Post, 88, 89
West Germany, 88
World War II, 32, 34, 39

Yanayev, Gennady, 16, 20, 21
Yazov, Dmitri, 16
Yeltsin, Anastasia "Naya" Girina (wife), 46, 47
Yeltsin, Boris Nikolayevich
   attempt on his life, 90
   baptism, 28, 29
   birth in Butko, Russia, 27
   as chairman of the Russian Supreme Soviet, 91, 92
   childhood, 32–40
   as Communist party member, 49, 53–59, 64–66
   as construction engineer, 43–47, 49, 53, 63, 64
   coup d'état, August 19, 1991, 11–25, 100, 102, 103
   disfigurement, 39
   education, 34–43, 62
   elected president of Russia, 97, 103, 106
   heads Moscow city committee, 65, 67
   heart trouble, 42–43, 75, 78
   love of volleyball, 38, 39, 40, 42, 63
   marriage, 46
   as minister of Gosstroi, 77
   as Politburo member, 59, 65, 68, 70, 103, 104
   resignation from the Politburo, 71, 73–77
   rivalry with Mikhail Gorbachev, 12, 25, 61–71, 87, 97, 99
Yeltsin, Klavdia Vasilievna Starygin (mother), 27, 32, 33
Yeltsin, Lena (daughter), 47
Yeltsin, Mikhail (brother), 27, 32
Yeltsin, Nikolai Ignatievich (father), 27, 30, 32, 33, 34, 35, 38, 41
Yeltsin, Tanya (daughter), 17, 47
Yeltsin, Valya (sister), 27, 32
"Yeltsin Affair, the," 73–77, 82, 85

PICTURE CREDITS

AP/Wide World Photos: pp. 22, 60, 72, 76, 87, 89, 94, 95, 96, 101, 104; The Bettmann Archive: p. 19; Culver Pictures: p. 31; Courtesy Andrew Nurnberg Associates, London: pp. 26, 36, 42, 45, 54; Reuters/Bettmann: pp. 2, 10, 12, 15, 16, 21, 24, 48, 57, 66, 69, 81, 84, 92, 98, 99, 103, 106; UPI/Bettmann: pp. 28, 30, 32, 35, 46, 51, 52, 62–63.

Kate Schecter is an assistant professor in political science at the University of Tel Aviv, Israel, where she specializes in the politics of health care in the former Soviet Union. She holds an M.A. in Soviet Studies from Harvard University and a Ph.D. in political science from Columbia University. Ms. Schecter is the coauthor of *An American Family in Moscow* (1975) and *Back in the U.S.S.R.* (1988) and has made three documentary films about the former Soviet Union. She is married to playwright Ari Roth and has one daughter, Isabel.

Vito Perrone is Director of Teacher Education and Chair of Teaching, Curriculum, and Learning Environments at Harvard University. He has previous experience as a public school teacher, a university professor of history, education, and peace studies (University of North Dakota), and as dean of the New School and the Center for Teaching and Learning (both at the University of North Dakota). Dr. Perrone has written extensively about such issues as educational equity, humanities curriculum, progressive education, and evaluation. His most recent books are: *A Letter to Teachers: Reflections on Schooling and the Art of Teaching*; *Enlarging Student Assessment in Schools*; *Working Papers: Reflections on Teachers, Schools, and Communities*; *Visions of Peace*; and *Johanna Knudsen Miller: A Pioneer Teacher*.

92
JB Yeltsin
Schecter, Kate.
  Boris Yeltsin

18.95

92
JB Yeltsin
Schecter, Kate.
  Boris Yeltsin

18.95

LAKEWOOD MEMORIAL LIBRARY
12 W. Summit Street
Lakewood, New York 14750

WITHDRAWN

**Member Of
Chautauqua-Cattaraugus Library System**